Oatmeal

101 recipes

Publications International, Ltd.

Copyright © 2011 Publications International, Ltd.

All rights reserved. This publication may not be reproduced or quoted in whole or in part by any means whatsoever without written permission from:

Louis Weber, CEO
Publications International, Ltd.
7373 North Cicero Avenue
Lincolnwood, IL 60712

Permission is never granted for commercial purposes.

Favorite Brand Name Recipes is a trademark of Publications International, Ltd.

All recipes and photographs that contain specific brand names are copyrighted by those companies and/or associations, unless otherwise specified. All photographs *except* those on pages 27, 49 and 81 copyright © Publications International, Ltd.

Carnation, Libby's, Nestlé and Toll House are registered trademarks of Nestlé

Some of the products listed in this publication may be in limited distribution.

Pictured on the front cover: Mixed Berry Crisp *(page 118)*.

Pictured on the back cover *(left to right):* Greek-Style Meatballs and Spinach *(page 122)* and Strawberry Muffins *(page 48)*.

ISBN-13: 978-1-4508-2163-6

ISBN-10: 1-4508-2163-4

Library of Congress Control Number: 2011921188

Manufactured in China.

8 7 6 5 4 3 2 1

Microwave Cooking: Microwave ovens vary in wattage. Use the cooking times as guidelines and check for doneness before adding more time.

Preparation/Cooking Times: Preparation times are based on the approximate amount of time required to assemble the recipe before cooking, baking, chilling or serving. These times include preparation steps such as measuring, chopping and mixing. The fact that some preparations and cooking can be done simultaneously is taken into account. Preparation of optional ingredients and serving suggestions is not included.

Publications International, Ltd.

table of contents

cherry-orange oatmeal
page 15

oatmeal-chip crispies
page 53

breakfast bites

oatmeal pecan pancakes
makes 4 servings

1¼ to 1½ **cups milk, divided**
½ **cup old-fashioned oats**
⅔ **cup all-purpose flour**
⅓ **cup whole wheat flour**
2½ **tablespoons packed light brown sugar**
2 **teaspoons baking powder**
½ **teaspoon baking soda**
¼ **teaspoon salt**
1 **egg**
2 **tablespoons melted butter**
½ **cup chopped toasted pecans**
Maple syrup

1. Bring ½ cup milk to a simmer in small saucepan. Stir in oats. Remove from heat; let stand 10 minutes.

2. Combine all-purpose flour, whole wheat flour, brown sugar, baking powder, baking soda and salt in large bowl; mix well.

3. Combine egg and butter in medium bowl; mix well. Stir in oatmeal and ¾ cup milk. Add to flour mixture; stir just until blended. *Do not beat.* If mixture is too thick, thin with remaining ¼ cup milk, 1 tablespoon at a time. Stir in pecans.

4. Lightly grease large skillet or griddle; heat over medium heat. Pour batter by ¼ cupfuls into skillet; flatten slightly. Cook 2 minutes or until tops are bubbly and bottoms are golden brown. Turn pancakes; cook 2 minutes more or until golden brown. Serve with maple syrup.

tip: To toast pecans, spread in single layer in small heavy skillet. Cook and stir over medium heat 2 to 4 minutes or until lightly browned. Remove from skillet immediately; cool before using.

winter trail mix
makes 12 servings

>   2 cups Old Fashioned QUAKER® Oats, uncooked
> 1½ cups QUAKER® Oatmeal Squares Cereal
>   ¼ cup maple-flavored syrup, regular or light
>   1 tablespoon vegetable oil
>   1 teaspoon vanilla
>   ½ cup snipped dried apple chunks
>   ½ cup snipped dried apricots
>   ½ cup dried cranberries
>   ¾ cup lightly salted almonds or dry-roasted peanuts

1. Heat oven to 325°F. Combine oats and cereal in large bowl. Combine maple syrup, oil and vanilla in small bowl; pour over cereal mixture. Mix until well coated. Transfer to 15×10-inch jelly-roll pan.

2. Bake 20 to 25 minutes until oats are golden brown, stirring every 10 minutes.

3. Remove from oven. Immediately stir in apples, apricots, cranberries and nuts. Cool completely in pan on wire rack. Store loosely covered up to 1 week.

serving suggestions: 1) Spread a whole-grain bagel half with peanut butter; sprinkle with trail mix, pressing lightly into peanut butter. 2) Mix trail mix with light cream cheese; spread on whole-grain bagels or whole-wheat toast. 3) Stir trail mix into low-fat vanilla yogurt or low-fat cottage cheese for breakfast or a snack. 4) Make a crunchy breakfast parfait by layering trail mix with fresh fruit (sliced bananas, chopped apples, grape halves, pineapple chunks) and low-fat yogurt. 5) Serve cold with milk. 6) Stir trail mix into pancake batter before cooking. 7) Put individual servings of trail mix in resealable plastic bags to eat away from home.

oatmeal with maple-glazed apples & cranberries

makes 4 servings

- **3 cups water**
- **¼ teaspoon salt**
- **2 cups quick or old-fashioned oats**
- **1 teaspoon butter**
- **¼ teaspoon ground cinnamon**
- **2 medium Red or Golden Delicious apples, unpeeled, cut into ½-inch chunks**
- **2 tablespoons maple syrup**
- **4 tablespoons dried cranberries**

1. Bring water and salt to a boil in large saucepan over high heat; stir in oats. Reduce heat to medium-low; simmer 1 to 2 minutes for quick oats or 5 to 6 minutes for old-fashioned oats.

2. Meanwhile, melt butter in medium nonstick skillet over medium heat. Stir in cinnamon. Add apples; cook and stir 4 to 5 minutes or until tender. Stir in maple syrup; heat through.

3. Spoon oatmeal into four bowls; top with apple mixture and cranberries.

date-nut granola
makes 6 cups

    2 cups old-fashioned oats
    2 cups barley flakes
    1 cup sliced almonds
 ⅓ cup vegetable oil
 ⅓ cup honey
    1 teaspoon vanilla
    1 cup chopped dates

1. Preheat oven to 350°F. Grease 13×9-inch baking pan.

2. Combine oats, barley flakes and almonds in large bowl.

3. Combine oil, honey and vanilla in small bowl. Pour honey mixture over oat mixture; stir until blended. Pour into prepared pan.

4. Bake about 25 minutes or until toasted, stirring frequently after first 10 minutes. Stir in dates while mixture is still hot. Cool completely; store in airtight container.

tip: You can find chopped dates in the supermarket where raisins and dried cranberries are sold. Or, purchase whole dates and chop them yourself—you'll need 5 to 6 ounces of dates to yield 1 cup chopped dates.

yummy breakfast cookies
makes about 4 dozen cookies

    1 cup all-purpose flour
 ¾ cup whole wheat flour
    1 teaspoon baking powder
    1 teaspoon baking soda
    1 teaspoon ground cinnamon
 ½ teaspoon salt
    1 cup (2 sticks) butter
    1 cup crunchy peanut butter
 ¾ cup granulated sugar
 ¾ cup packed brown sugar
    2 eggs
    1 teaspoon vanilla
1¾ cups quick oats
1¼ cups raisins
    1 medium Granny Smith apple, finely grated
 ⅓ cup finely grated carrot

1. Preheat oven to 350°F. Combine all-purpose flour, whole wheat flour, baking powder, baking soda, cinnamon and salt in medium bowl.

2. Beat butter, peanut butter, granulated sugar and brown sugar in large bowl with electric mixer at medium speed 2 minutes or until light and fluffy. Add eggs; beat 1 minute. Add flour mixture; beat at low speed until blended. Stir in oats, raisins, apple and carrot. Drop dough by tablespoonfuls onto ungreased cookie sheets.

3. Bake 12 to 15 minutes or just until browned around edges. *Do not overbake.* Cool cookies on cookie sheets 2 minutes; remove to wire racks to cool completely.

tip: Freeze cookies between sheets of waxed paper in an airtight container. Thaw cookies for a breakfast on the run or for a nutritious snack.

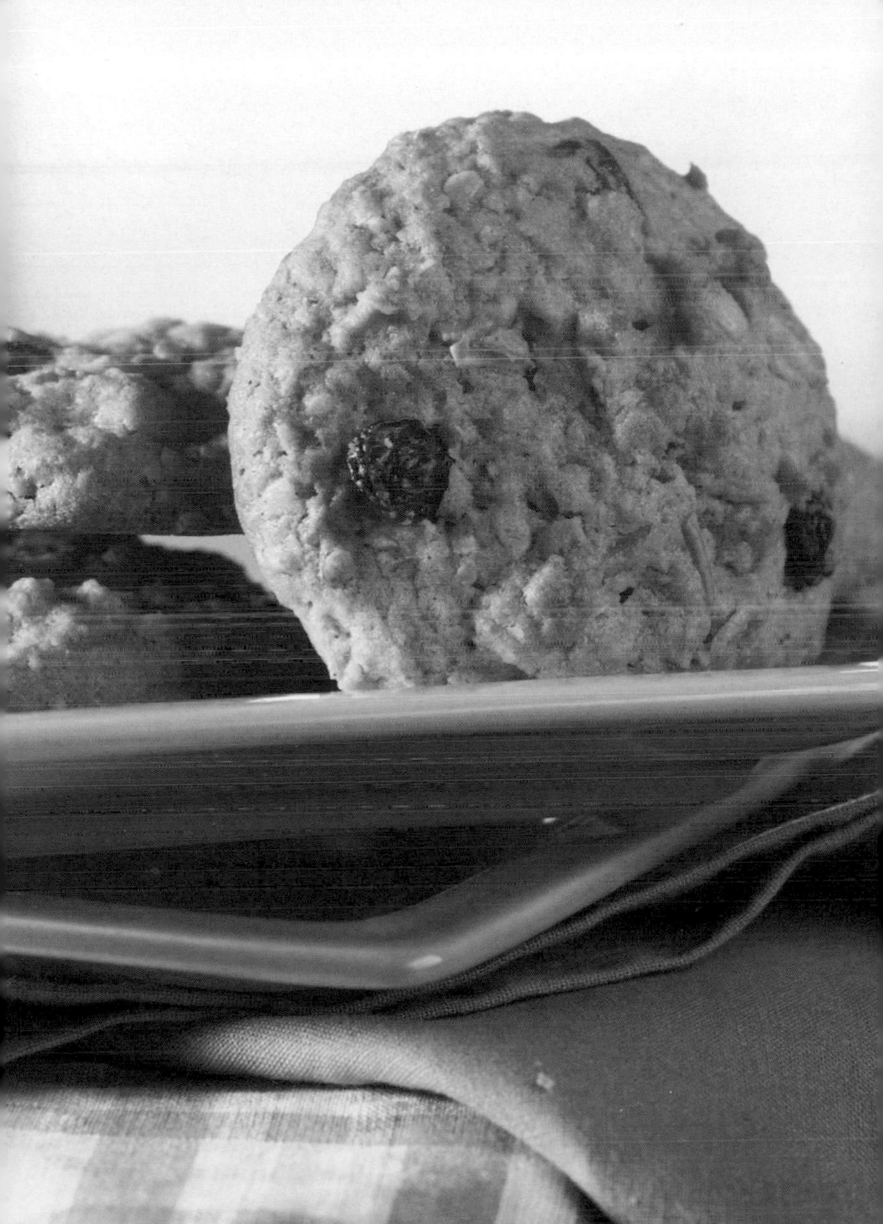

sunny seed bran waffles
makes 4 waffles

     2 egg whites
     1 tablespoon dark brown sugar
     1 tablespoon vegetable oil
     1 cup milk
   2/3 cup wheat bran
   2/3 cup quick oats
  1½ teaspoons baking powder
   ¼ teaspoon salt
     3 tablespoons sunflower seeds, toasted*
     1 cup apple butter

To toast sunflower seeds, cook and stir in small nonstick skillet over medium heat about 5 minutes or until golden brown. Remove from skillet; let cool.

1. Beat egg whites in medium bowl with electric mixer until soft peaks form. Blend brown sugar and oil in small bowl. Stir in milk; mix well.

2. Combine bran, oats, baking powder and salt in large bowl; mix well. Stir milk mixture into bran mixture. Add sunflower seeds; stir just until moistened. *Do not overmix.* Gently fold in beaten egg whites.

3. Spray nonstick waffle iron lightly with nonstick cooking spray; heat according to manufacturer's directions. Stir batter; spoon ½ cup batter into waffle iron for each waffle. Cook until steam stops escaping from around edges and waffle is golden brown. Serve each waffle with ¼ cup apple butter.

note: It is essential to use a nonstick waffle iron because of the low fat content of these waffles.

oat cakes with raspberry topping

makes 6 servings

  1 pint raspberries, divided
½ cup sugar, divided
  2 tablespoons cornstarch
½ cup water
  1 teaspoon lemon juice
½ cup quick oats
  1 cup whole wheat flour
2½ teaspoons baking powder
1¼ cups milk
½ cup plain yogurt

1. Place half of raspberries in medium bowl; mash with potato masher.

2. Combine ⅓ cup sugar and cornstarch in small saucepan. Stir in water until smooth. Cook and stir over medium heat until mixture comes to a boil. Add lemon juice and mashed raspberries; return to a boil. Remove from heat; let stand 15 minutes. Gently stir in remaining whole raspberries.

3. Cook and stir oats in small skillet over medium heat 3 minutes or until slightly browned. Place in medium bowl; cool 10 minutes. Stir in flour, baking powder and remaining sugar. Combine milk and yogurt in small bowl; stir into flour mixture just until dry ingredients are moistened. (Batter will be lumpy.)

4. Spray nonstick griddle or large skillet with nonstick cooking spray; heat over medium heat until water droplets sprinkled on griddle bounce off surface. Drop batter by scant ¼ cupfuls onto griddle; spread batter to form 4-inch round cakes. Cook 2 minutes or until top is covered with bubbles. Turn cakes; cook 2 minutes more or until browned. Serve warm with raspberry topping.

variation: Substitute sliced hulled strawberries or blueberries for the raspberries. Mash half the berries and leave the rest whole.

cherry-orange oatmeal
makes 4 servings

1 can (11 ounces) mandarin orange
    segments in light syrup, drained,
    divided
1 cup fresh pitted cherries or frozen
    dark sweet cherries, divided
2 cups water
1 cup old-fashioned oats
2 tablespoons sugar
1 tablespoon unsweetened cocoa powder

1. Set aside ¼ cup orange segments and ¼ cup cherries for garnish.

2. Combine water, remaining orange segments, remaining cherries, oats, sugar and cocoa in medium microwavable bowl or 1½-quart casserole. Microwave on HIGH 2 minutes. Stir; microwave 4 minutes.

3. Divide mixture evenly among four serving bowls. Garnish with reserved oranges and cherries.

> **tip:** Use the tip of a swivel-bladed vegetable peeler
> or a small knife inserted through the stem end of
> a cherry to remove the pit. If you cook and bake
> frequently with cherries, you might want to purchase
> a cherry pitter, an inexpensive tool that holds a single
> cherry while a plunger pushes out the pit.

chunky-fruity homemade granola
makes 8 cups

>   2 cups old-fashioned oats
>   1⅓ cups slivered almonds
>   1 cup shredded coconut
>   3 tablespoons unsalted butter
>   ¼ cup honey
>   1 cup chopped dried apricots
>   ¾ cup dried cranberries
>   ¾ cup dried tart cherries
>   ½ cup dried blueberries
>   ½ cup roasted unsalted cashew pieces

1. Preheat oven to 300°F. Line large baking sheet with foil or parchment paper.

2. Combine oats, almonds and coconut in large bowl. Place butter in small microwavable bowl; microwave on HIGH 30 to 45 seconds or until melted. Whisk in honey until blended. Pour butter mixture over oat mixture; toss to coat. Transfer mixture to prepared baking sheet, spreading evenly.

3. Bake 20 to 25 minutes or until golden, stirring once or twice during baking. Cool mixture in pan on wire rack.

4. Combine apricots, cranberries, cherries, blueberries and cashews in large bowl. Crumble cooled oat mixture into fruit mixture; stir until blended. Store granola in airtight container.

serving suggestions: Layer granola with yogurt for parfaits, sprinkle it over ice cream or portion it into resealable food storage bags for an on-the-go snack.

slow cooker oatmeal
makes 6 servings

> **3 cups water**
> **2 cups chopped peeled apples**
> **1½ cups steel-cut or old-fashioned oats**
> **¼ cup sliced almonds**
> **½ teaspoon ground cinnamon**

slow cooker directions
Combine water, apples, oats, almonds and cinnamon in slow cooker. Cover; cook on LOW 8 hours.

raisin-nut oatmeal
makes 4 servings

> **3¾ cups water**
> **2⅔ cups old-fashioned oats**
> **⅔ cup raisins**
> **½ cup sliced almonds, toasted***
> **⅓ cup nonfat dry milk powder**
> **⅓ cup packed light brown sugar**
> **½ teaspoon salt**
> **½ teaspoon ground cinnamon**
> **⅛ teaspoon ground ginger**

To toast almonds, spread in single layer in small heavy skillet. Cook and stir over medium heat about 2 minutes or until golden brown.

1. Bring water to a boil in large saucepan over high heat. Stir in oats, raisins, almonds, milk powder, brown sugar, salt, cinnamon and ginger.

2. Reduce heat to medium; cook and stir 4 to 5 minutes or until oatmeal is thick and creamy.

hearty banana oat flapjacks

makes 12 (4-inch) pancakes

2 large ripe bananas, peeled and sliced
1 tablespoon granulated sugar
1 cup all-purpose flour
½ cup QUAKER® Oats (quick or old fashioned, uncooked)
1 tablespoon baking powder
¼ teaspoon ground cinnamon
¼ teaspoon salt (optional)
1 cup fat-free (skim) milk
1 egg, lightly beaten
2 tablespoons vegetable oil
AUNT JEMIMA® Syrup, warmed
Additional banana slices (optional)
Coarsely chopped pecans or walnuts (optional)

1. Combine banana slices and sugar in medium bowl; stir to coat slices with sugar. Set aside.

2. Combine flour, oats, baking powder, cinnamon and salt, if desired, in large bowl; mix well. Combine milk, egg and oil in medium bowl; blend well. Add to dry ingredients all at once; stir just until dry ingredients are moistened. (Do not overmix.)

3. Heat griddle over medium-high heat (or preheat electric skillet or griddle to 375°F). Lightly grease griddle. For each pancake, pour scant ¼ cup batter onto hot griddle. Top with four or five sugar-coated banana slices. Turn pancakes when tops are covered with bubbles and edges look cooked.

4. Serve with warm syrup and additional banana slices and nuts, if desired.

granola breakfast cookies

makes 1½ dozen cookies

- 1½ **cups old-fashioned oats**
- ½ **cup all-purpose flour**
- ½ **cup roasted salted sunflower seeds**
- ½ **cup dried cranberries**
- ¼ **cup packed light brown sugar**
- ½ **teaspoon baking powder**
- ¼ **cup peanut butter**
- 2 **eggs**
- ¼ **cup honey**
- 1 **teaspoon vanilla**

1. Preheat oven to 350°F. Line cookie sheets with parchment paper.

2. Combine oats, flour, sunflower seeds, cranberries, brown sugar and baking powder in large bowl; mix well. Microwave peanut butter in medium microwavable bowl on HIGH 30 to 40 seconds or until slightly melted. Whisk in eggs, honey and vanilla until well blended. Add to oat mixture; mix well.

3. Drop dough by tablespoonfuls onto prepared cookie sheets; flatten slightly to 3-inch diameter with bottom of glass sprayed with nonstick cooking spray.

4. Bake 15 to 17 minutes or until bottoms of cookies are light golden brown. Remove to wire racks to cool completely. Store cookies in airtight container up to 1 week.

serving suggestion: Dip cookies into yogurt topped with diced fresh fruit.

fruited granola
makes about 20 servings

3 cups quick oats
1 cup sliced almonds
1 cup honey
½ cup wheat germ or honey wheat germ
3 tablespoons butter, melted
1 teaspoon ground cinnamon
3 cups whole grain cereal flakes
½ cup dried blueberries or golden raisins
½ cup dried cranberries or cherries
½ cup dried banana chips or chopped pitted dates

1. Preheat oven to 325°F.

2. Spread oats and almonds in single layer in 13×9-inch baking pan. Bake 15 minutes or until lightly toasted, stirring frequently.

3. Combine honey, wheat germ, butter and cinnamon in large bowl until well blended. Add oats and almonds; toss to coat completely. Spread mixture in single layer in baking pan. Bake 20 minutes or until golden brown. Cool completely in pan on wire rack. Break mixture into chunks.

4. Combine oat chunks, cereal, blueberries, cranberries and banana chips in large bowl; mix well. Store in airtight container at room temperature up to 2 weeks.

microwave oats cereal
makes 2 servings

- 1¾ **cups water**
- ⅓ **cup old-fashioned oats**
- ⅓ **cup oat bran**
- 1 **tablespoon brown sugar**
- ¼ **teaspoon ground cinnamon**
- ⅛ **teaspoon salt**

1. Combine water, oats, oat bran, brown sugar, cinnamon and salt in large microwavable bowl (cereal expands rapidly when it cooks). Cover with vented plastic wrap.

2. Microwave on HIGH about 6 minutes or until thickened. Stir well. Let stand 2 minutes before serving.

serving suggestion: To boost the flavor and nutrition of this quick morning meal, top with fresh blueberries or strawberries, or stir in chopped nuts and dried cherries.

> **tip:** Oat bran is found in rolled oats and steel-cut oats, but it may also be purchased as a separate product—look for it in bags or boxes in the cereal or baking section of supermarkets and natural food stores.

orange cinnamon pancakes
makes 12 pancakes

- **2 cups old-fashioned oats**
- **2 cups orange juice**
- **¼ cup whole wheat pastry flour**
- **1 teaspoon baking powder**
- **½ teaspoon baking soda**
- **½ teaspoon salt**
- **½ teaspoon ground cinnamon**
- **2 eggs, lightly beaten**
- **¼ cup canola oil**
- **2 tablespoons honey**
- **2 teaspoons grated orange peel**
- **Plain yogurt and orange slices (optional)**

1. Combine oats and orange juice in large bowl; mix well. Cover and refrigerate 30 minutes or overnight.

2. Sift flour, baking powder, baking soda, salt and cinnamon into oat mixture. Add eggs, oil, honey and orange peel; stir just until blended.

3. Spray nonstick griddle or large skillet with nonstick cooking spray; heat over medium-low heat. Spoon batter by ¼ cupfuls onto hot griddle. Cook 2 to 3 minutes or until bubbles appear. Turn pancakes; cook until lightly browned. Garnish with yogurt and orange slices.

rise and shine sausage oatmeal cups

makes 12 sausage cups

oatmeal cups
- 1 pound BOB EVANS® Original Recipe Roll Sausage
- ⅔ cup quick or old-fashioned oats
- ¼ cup milk
- 1 egg white
- 1 tablespoon finely chopped onion

filling
- 2 teaspoons butter
- 8 eggs, beaten
- ½ cup soft cream cheese (plain or herb)
- ¾ cup chopped seeded tomato, drained
- 2 tablespoons snipped fresh chives, fresh dill or green onion tops
- Salt and black pepper to taste

Preheat oven to 350°F. To prepare oatmeal cups, combine sausage, oats, milk, egg white and onion in medium bowl. Divide mixture evenly among 12 muffin pan cups. Press mixture firmly on bottom and up sides to form hollow cups. Bake 12 to 15 minutes or until cooked through. Drain cups on paper towels and keep warm.

To prepare filling, melt butter in large skillet. Add eggs; cook, stirring frequently. When almost done, fold in remaining ingredients; cook until eggs reach desired doneness. Divide mixture evenly among sausage cups; serve hot. Refrigerate leftovers.

note: Sausage cups can be prepared in advance and refrigerated overnight or frozen up to 1 month. Reheat when ready to fill.

berry power drink
makes 2 servings

1 cup fruit juice (such as orange, cranberry or apple)
1 cup fresh or frozen strawberries
1 container (8 ounces) low-fat vanilla yogurt
⅔ cup QUAKER® Oats (quick or old fashioned, uncooked)
1 cup ice cubes
Granulated sugar, to taste

1. Place juice, strawberries, yogurt and oats in blender container. Cover, blend on HIGH speed about 2 minutes or until smooth.

2. Gradually add ice; blend on HIGH speed an additional minute or until smooth. Blend in sugar to taste.

3. Serve immediately.

cherry "pie" oatmeal
makes 4 to 5 servings

4 cups water
3 cups old-fashioned oats
⅔ cup nonfat dry milk powder
½ cup dried cherries
⅓ cup lightly packed dark brown sugar
½ teaspoon salt
Milk (optional)

1. Bring water to a boil in large saucepan over high heat. Stir in oats, milk powder, cherries, brown sugar and salt.

2. Reduce heat to medium-high; cook and stir 4 to 5 minutes or until thick and creamy. Serve with milk, if desired.

mixed berry whole grain coffee cake
makes 12 servings

- 1¼ cups all-purpose flour, divided
- ¾ cup quick oats
- ¾ cup packed light brown sugar
- 3 tablespoons butter, softened
- 1 cup whole wheat flour
- 1 cup milk
- ¾ cup granulated sugar
- ¼ cup canola oil
- 1 egg, slightly beaten
- 1 tablespoon baking powder
- 1 teaspoon ground cinnamon
- ½ teaspoon salt
- 1½ cups frozen unsweetened mixed berries, thawed and drained
  or 2 cups fresh berries
- ¼ cup chopped walnuts

1. Preheat oven to 350°F. Spray 9×5-inch loaf pan with nonstick cooking spray.

2. Combine ¼ cup all-purpose flour, oats, brown sugar and butter in small bowl; mix with fork until crumbly.

3. Beat remaining 1 cup all-purpose flour, whole wheat flour, milk, granulated sugar, oil, egg, baking powder, cinnamon and salt in large bowl with electric mixer until well blended (or whisk 1 to 2 minutes). Gently fold in berries. Spread batter in prepared pan; sprinkle evenly with oat mixture and walnuts.

4. Bake 38 to 40 minutes or until toothpick inserted into center comes out clean. Serve warm.

fruit and oat scones
makes 10 scones

1½ cups all-purpose flour
1 cup QUAKER® Oats (quick or old fashioned, uncooked)
Heat-stable sugar substitute equal to 3 tablespoons sugar
1½ teaspoons baking powder
½ teaspoon baking soda
½ teaspoon ground cinnamon
¼ teaspoon salt (optional)
5 tablespoons margarine, chilled and cut into pieces
⅓ cup finely chopped dried mixed fruit, dried cranberries or raisins
⅔ cup low-fat buttermilk
¼ cup egg substitute or 2 egg whites, lightly beaten

1. Heat oven to 400°F. Lightly spray cookie sheet with nonstick cooking spray.

2. Combine flour, oats, sugar substitute, baking powder, baking soda, cinnamon and salt, if desired, in large bowl; mix well. Cut in margarine with pastry blender or two knives until mixture resembles coarse crumbs. Stir in dried fruit. Add combined buttermilk and egg substitute to dry ingredients all at once; stir with fork just until dry ingredients are moistened. (Do not overmix.)

3. Drop dough by ¼ cup portions 2 inches apart onto cookie sheet. Bake 12 to 15 minutes or until very light golden brown. Serve warm.

cranberry-oatmeal mini muffins

makes 24 mini muffins

  1 cup quick oats
  ¾ cup milk
  1 egg, beaten
  2 tablespoons butter, melted
  1 cup all-purpose flour
  ⅓ cup packed brown sugar
  1 tablespoon baking powder
  ½ teaspoon baking soda
  ½ teaspoon ground cinnamon
  ¼ teaspoon salt
  ½ cup finely chopped dried cranberries *or* **¼ cup finely chopped**
    dried cranberries and ¼ cup finely chopped walnuts

1. Preheat oven to 375°F. Generously grease 24 mini (1¾-inch) muffin cups.

2. Combine oats and milk in large bowl; stir and set aside 5 minutes to soak. Stir in egg and butter until blended.

3. Combine flour, brown sugar, baking powder, baking soda, cinnamon and salt in small bowl. Stir flour mixture into oat mixture just until dry ingredients are moistened. *Do not overmix.* Stir in cranberries. Spoon batter into prepared pans, filling three-fourths full.

4. Bake 12 to 15 minutes or until toothpick inserted into centers comes out clean. Cool muffins in pans 1 minute; remove to wire racks to cool completely.

crunchy whole grain bread
makes 2 loaves

     2 cups warm water (105°F to 115°F), divided
    1/3 cup honey
     2 tablespoons vegetable oil
     1 tablespoon salt
     2 packages (1/4 ounce each) active dry yeast
     2 to 21/2 cups whole wheat flour, divided
     1 cup bread flour
    11/4 cups quick oats, divided
    1/2 cup hulled pumpkin seeds or sunflower kernels
    1/2 cup assorted grains and seeds
     1 egg white
     1 tablespoon water

1. Combine 11/2 cups water, honey, oil and salt in small saucepan. Cook and stir over low heat until warm (115°F to 120°F).

2. Dissolve yeast in remaining 1/2 cup water in bowl of electric stand mixer; let stand 5 minutes. Stir in honey mixture. Add 1 cup whole wheat flour and bread flour; knead with dough hook at low speed 2 minutes or until combined. Gradually add 1 cup oats, pumpkin seeds and assorted grains. Add remaining whole wheat flour, 1/2 cup at a time, until dough begins to form a ball. Continue kneading 7 to 10 minutes or until dough is smooth and elastic.

3. Place dough in lightly oiled bowl, turning to coat top. Cover loosely with plastic wrap; let rise in warm place 11/2 to 2 hours or until doubled in bulk.

4. Grease two 9×5-inch loaf pans. Punch down dough. Divide in half. Shape each half into loaf; place in prepared pans. Cover with plastic wrap; let rise in warm place 1 hour or until almost doubled in bulk.

5. Preheat oven to 375°F. Whisk egg white and water in small bowl. Brush tops of loaves with egg mixture; sprinkle with remaining 1/4 cup oats. Bake 35 to 45 minutes or until loaves sound hollow when tapped. Cool loaves in pans 10 minutes; remove to wire rack to cool completely.

carrot and oat muffins

makes 12 muffins

- ½ **cup milk**
- ½ **cup unsweetened applesauce**
- 2 **eggs, beaten**
- 1 **tablespoon canola oil**
- ½ **cup shredded carrot (1 medium to large carrot)**
- ¾ **cup plus 2 tablespoons old-fashioned oats**
- ¾ **cup all-purpose flour**
- ¾ **cup whole wheat flour**
- ⅓ **cup sugar**
- 1½ **teaspoons baking powder**
- 1 **teaspoon ground cinnamon**
- ½ **teaspoon baking soda**
- ¼ **teaspoon salt**
- ¼ **cup finely chopped walnuts (optional)**

1. Preheat oven to 350°F. Spray 12 standard (2½-inch) muffin cups with nonstick cooking spray.

2. Whisk milk, applesauce, eggs and oil in large bowl until blended. Stir in carrot. Combine oats, all-purpose flour, whole wheat flour, sugar, baking powder, cinnamon, baking soda and salt in medium bowl; mix well. Add flour mixture to applesauce mixture; stir just until batter is moistened. *Do not overmix.*

3. Spoon batter into prepared muffin cups, filling two-thirds to three-fourths full. Sprinkle 1 teaspoon walnuts over each muffin, if desired.

4. Bake 20 to 22 minutes or until muffins are golden brown. Cool muffins in pan 5 minutes; remove to wire rack to cool completely.

note: These muffins are best eaten the same day they are made.

soft oaty pretzels
makes 24 pretzels

    3 to 3½ cups all-purpose flour, divided
1½ cups QUAKER® Oats (quick or
        old fashioned, uncooked), divided
    2 tablespoons granulated sugar
    1 package (¼ ounce) quick-rising yeast
        (about 2¼ teaspoons)
1½ teaspoons salt
 ¾ cup milk
 ¾ cup water
    2 tablespoons margarine or butter, softened
    1 egg, lightly beaten

1. Combine 2 cups flour, 1¼ cups oats, sugar, yeast and salt in large bowl; mix well. Heat milk and water in small saucepan until very warm (120°F to 130°F); stir in margarine. Add to flour mixture. Blend with electric mixer at low speed until moistened; beat 3 minutes at medium speed. By hand, gradually stir in enough remaining flour to make soft dough that pulls away from sides of bowl.

2. Turn dough out onto lightly floured surface. Knead 5 to 8 minutes or until smooth and elastic, adding additional flour if dough is sticky. Cover loosely with plastic wrap; let dough rest on floured surface 10 minutes.

3. Heat oven to 350°F. Lightly grease or spray two large baking sheets with nonstick cooking spray.

4. Divide dough into 24 equal pieces. Roll each piece into 12-inch-long rope; form into pretzel, letter or number shape. Place on baking sheet. Cover loosely with plastic wrap; let rest 10 minutes or until slightly risen. Brush tops of pretzel with beaten egg; sprinkle with remaining ¼ cup oats, pressing lightly.

5. Bake 15 to 18 minutes or until golden brown. (If baking both sheets at one time, rotate sheets top to bottom and front to back halfway through baking time.) Remove from baking sheets; cool on wire racks. Store tightly covered at room temperature.

plum oatmeal muffins
makes 18 muffins

    5 fresh California plums, halved and pitted, divided
    2 cups all-purpose flour
1¾ cups rolled oats
    ¾ cup packed brown sugar
    ⅓ cup vegetable oil
    1 egg
    1 tablespoon baking powder
    1 teaspoon salt
    1 teaspoon vanilla
    1 teaspoon grated orange peel

Spray nonstick cooking spray in muffin cups or use paper liners.
Preheat oven to 350°F. Cut up 3 plums to measure 1 cup. Add to food
processor or blender; process until smooth. Coarsely chop remaining
2 plums; set aside. Combine puréed plums, flour, oats, brown sugar,
oil, egg, baking powder, salt, vanilla and orange peel. Stir until just
blended. Stir in chopped plums. Fill prepared muffin cups ⅔ full.
Bake 30 to 35 minutes or until wooden toothpick inserted in center
comes out clean.

*Favorite recipe from **California Tree Fruit Agreement***

strawberry banana bread

makes 16 servings

Nonstick cooking spray
1 cup oats
½ cup fat-free milk
1 cup mashed very ripe bananas (about 2 medium)
½ cup cholesterol-free egg substitute
½ cup canola oil
2 cups all-purpose flour
2 tablespoons sugar substitute for baking or ¼ cup sugar
2 teaspoons baking powder
½ teaspoon baking soda
½ teaspoon salt
½ cup POLANER® Sugar Free Strawberry or Sugar Free Blueberry Preserves

Heat oven to 350°F. Lightly coat bottom only of 8×4-inch loaf pan with nonstick cooking spray.

Combine oats and milk in medium bowl; mix well. Let stand 10 minutes. Stir in bananas, egg substitute and oil until combined.

Combine flour, sugar substitute, baking powder, baking soda and salt in large bowl; mix well. Add banana mixture to dry ingredients all at once; stir just until ingredients are moistened.

Stir preserves in small bowl until thinned to spreading consistency.

Pour half of batter into prepared pan; spoon preserves over batter, spreading to cover. Spoon remaining batter evenly over preserves.

Bake 55 to 60 minutes or until wooden pick inserted in center comes out clean. Cool in pan on wire rack 10 minutes. Remove from pan. Cool completely.

tip: Store banana bread, tightly wrapped in plastic wrap or foil, at room temperature. Freeze for longer storage.

tip: This special banana bread makes a great hostess gift. Wrap in decorative foil or colored plastic wrap, tuck in a basket or onto a cutting board and add a jar of sugar free preserves.

cinnamon oat rolls
makes 9 rolls

**1 pound frozen bread dough, thawed
    according to package directions**
**1 cup QUAKER® Oats (quick or
    old fashioned, uncooked)**
⅓ cup firmly packed brown sugar
2 teaspoons ground cinnamon
**⅓ cup (5 tablespoons plus 1 teaspoon)
    margarine or butter, melted**
¾ cup raisins or dried cranberries
¼ cup orange marmalade

1. Let dough stand, covered, at room temperature 15 minutes to relax. Spray 8- or 9-inch square baking pan with nonstick cooking spray.

2. Combine oats, brown sugar and cinnamon in medium bowl. Add margarine; mix well. Stir in raisins. Set aside.

3. Roll dough into 12×10-inch rectangle. (Dough will be very elastic.) Spread evenly with oat mixture to within ½ inch of edges. Starting from long side, roll up; pinch seam to seal. With sharp knife, cut into 9 slices about 1¼ inches wide; place in prepared pan, cut sides down. Cover loosely with plastic wrap; let rise in warm place 30 minutes or until nearly doubled in size.

4. Heat oven to 350°F. Bake 30 to 35 minutes or until golden brown. Cool 5 minutes in pan on wire rack; remove from pan. Spread tops of rolls with marmalade. Serve warm.

oat raisin bread
makes 2 loaves (12 servings each)

- 1½ cups all-purpose flour
- 1 cup whole wheat flour
- 1 cup uncooked quick or old-fashioned oats
- 2 teaspoons baking soda
- ½ teaspoon salt
- 1½ cups buttermilk
- 2 eggs
- ½ cup KARO® Light or Dark Corn Syrup
- ½ cup packed brown sugar
- ¼ cup MAZOLA® Oil
- 1 cup raisins

1. Preheat oven to 350°F. Grease and flour 2 (9×5×3-inch) loaf pans.

2. In large bowl combine flours, oats, baking soda and salt.

3. In small bowl combine buttermilk, eggs, corn syrup, brown sugar and oil until blended. Stir into flour mixture just until moistened. Stir in raisins. Pour batter into prepared pans.

4. Bake 45 to 50 minutes or until toothpick inserted into centers comes out clean. Cool in pans 10 minutes. Remove from pans; cool on wire rack.

prep time: 15 minutes • **bake time:** 50 minutes, plus cooling

oat and whole wheat scones

makes 8 servings

    1 cup old-fashioned oats
    1 cup whole wheat flour
    ½ cup all-purpose flour
    ¼ cup sugar
    1 tablespoon baking powder
    ¼ teaspoon salt
    ½ cup (1 stick) unsalted butter, cut into small pieces
    ½ cup whipping cream
    1 egg
    ¾ cup dried cherries

1. Preheat oven to 425°F. Line baking sheet with parchment paper.

2. Combine oats, whole wheat flour, all-purpose flour, sugar, baking powder and salt in large bowl. Cut in butter with pastry blender or two forks until mixture resembles coarse crumbs.

3. Whisk cream and egg in small bowl until blended. Stir into flour mixture until dough comes together. Stir in cherries.

4. Transfer dough to lightly floured surface. Shape dough into 8-inch disc about ¾ inch thick. Cut disc into 8 wedges. Arrange wedges in round shape on prepared baking sheet, leaving 1 inch between wedges.

5. Bake 15 minutes. Spread wedges apart on baking sheet, leaving 2 inches between wedges. Bake 3 to 5 minutes. Serve warm.

oatmeal pumpkin bread
makes one loaf (16 slices)

- **1 cup quick-cooking oats**
- **1 cup low-fat milk, heated**
- **¾ cup cooked or canned pumpkin**
- **2 eggs, beaten**
- **¼ cup margarine, melted**
- **2 cups all-purpose flour**
- **1 cup sugar**
- **1 tablespoon baking powder**
- **1 teaspoon ground cinnamon**
- **¼ teaspoon ground nutmeg**
- **¼ teaspoon salt**
- **1 cup raisins**
- **½ cup chopped pecans**

Preheat oven to 350°F. In large bowl, combine oats and milk; let stand about 5 minutes. Stir in pumpkin, eggs and margarine. In separate bowl, mix together flour, sugar, baking powder, cinnamon, nutmeg and salt. Gradually add dry ingredients to oatmeal mixture. Stir in raisins and nuts; mix well. Place in greased 9×5-inch loaf pan. Bake 55 to 60 minutes or until done. Cool on wire rack.

*Favorite recipe from **The Sugar Association, Inc.***

wisconsin cheddar cheese scones
makes 8 to 12 scones

- 1½ cups all-purpose flour
- 1½ cups uncooked quick-cooking oats
- ¼ cup packed brown sugar
- 1 tablespoon baking powder
- 1 teaspoon cream of tartar
- ½ teaspoon salt
- ½ cup (2 ounces) finely shredded Wisconsin Cheddar cheese
- ⅔ cup butter, melted
- ⅓ cup milk
- 1 egg

Preheat oven to 425°F. Stir together flour, oats, brown sugar, baking powder, cream of tartar and salt in large bowl. Stir in cheese. Beat together butter, milk and egg in small bowl. Add to dry ingredients, stirring just until mixed. Shape dough into ball; pat onto lightly floured surface to form 8-inch circle. Cut into 8 to 12 wedges. Bake on buttered baking sheet 12 to 15 minutes until light golden brown.

Favorite recipe from **Wisconsin Milk Marketing Board**

tip: To avoid tough, dense or heavy scones, don't work the dough too much—mix only until the ingredients are incorporated but just barely hold together.

quaker's best oatmeal bread

makes 2 loaves (32 servings)

5¾ to 6¼ **cups all-purpose flour, divided**
2½ **cups QUAKER® Oats (quick or old fashioned, uncooked)**
¼ **cup granulated sugar**
2 **packages (¼ ounce each) quick-rising yeast (about**
4½ **teaspoons)**
2½ **teaspoons salt**
1½ **cups water**
1¼ **cups fat-free (skim) milk**
¼ **cup (½ stick) margarine or butter**

1. Combine 3 cups flour, oats, sugar, yeast and salt in large bowl; mix well. Heat water, milk and margarine in small saucepan until very warm (120°F to 130°F). Add to flour mixture. Blend with electric mixer on low speed until dry ingredients are moistened. Increase to medium speed; beat 3 minutes. By hand, gradually stir in enough remaining flour to make stiff dough.

2. Turn dough out onto lightly floured surface. Knead 5 to 8 minutes or until smooth and elastic. Shape dough into ball; place in greased bowl, turning once. Cover; let rise in warm place 30 minutes or until doubled in size.

3. Punch down dough. Cover; let rest 10 minutes. Divide dough in half; shape to form loaves. Place in two greased 8×4-inch or 9×5-inch loaf pans. Cover; let rise in warm place 15 minutes or until nearly doubled in size.

4. Heat oven to 375°F. Bake 45 to 50 minutes or until dark golden brown. Remove from pans to wire rack. Cool completely before slicing.

tip: If desired, brush tops of loaves lightly with melted margarine or butter and sprinkle with additional oats after placing in pans.

strawberry muffins
makes 12 muffins

1¼ cups all-purpose flour
2½ teaspoons baking powder
½ teaspoon salt
1 cup old-fashioned oats
½ cup sugar
1 cup milk
½ cup (1 stick) butter, melted
1 egg, beaten
1 teaspoon vanilla
1 cup chopped fresh strawberries

1. Preheat oven to 425°F. Grease bottoms only of 12 standard (2½-inch) muffin cups or line with paper baking cups.

2. Combine flour, baking powder and salt in large bowl. Stir in oats and sugar. Combine milk, butter, egg and vanilla in small bowl until well blended; stir into flour mixture just until moistened. Fold in strawberries. Spoon into prepared muffin cups, filling about two-thirds full.

3. Bake 15 to 18 minutes or until lightly browned and toothpick inserted into centers comes out clean. Remove muffins from pan; cool on wire rack 10 minutes. Serve warm or cool completely.

cranberry oat bread
makes 2 loaves

- ¾ cup honey
- 2 eggs
- ½ cup milk
- ⅓ cup vegetable oil
- 2½ cups all-purpose flour
- 1 cup quick-cooking rolled oats
- 1 teaspoon baking soda
- 1 teaspoon baking powder
- ½ teaspoon salt
- ½ teaspoon ground cinnamon
- 2 cups fresh or frozen cranberries
- 1 cup chopped nuts

Combine honey, eggs, milk and oil in large bowl; mix well. Combine flour, oats, baking soda, baking powder, salt and cinnamon in medium bowl; mix well. Stir into honey mixture. Fold in cranberries and nuts. Spoon into 2 greased and floured 8½×4½×2½-inch loaf pans.

Bake in preheated 350°F oven 40 to 45 minutes or until wooden toothpick inserted near centers comes out clean. Cool in pans on wire racks 15 minutes. Remove from pans; cool completely on wire racks.

Favorite recipe from **National Honey Board**

cookie jar favorites

peanut butter jumbos
makes 1½ dozen cookies

- **1½ cups peanut butter**
- **1 cup granulated sugar**
- **1 cup packed brown sugar**
- **3 eggs**
- **½ cup (1 stick) butter, softened**
- **1 teaspoon vanilla**
- **4½ cups old-fashioned oats**
- **2 teaspoons baking soda**
- **1 cup (6 ounces) semisweet chocolate chips**
- **1 cup candy-coated chocolate pieces**

1. Preheat oven to 350°F. Lightly grease cookie sheets or line with parchment paper.

2. Beat peanut butter, granulated sugar, brown sugar, eggs, butter and vanilla in large bowl with electric mixer until well blended. Stir in oats and baking soda until well blended. Stir in chocolate chips and chocolate pieces.

3. Drop dough by ⅓ cupfuls about 4 inches apart onto prepared cookie sheets. Press each cookie to flatten slightly.

4. Bake 15 to 20 minutes or until firm in center. Remove cookies to wire racks to cool completely.

peanut butter jumbo sandwiches: Prepare cookies as directed. Place ⅓ cup softened chocolate or vanilla ice cream on bottom of one cookie. Top with second cookie; lightly press sandwich together. Repeat with remaining cookies. Wrap sandwiches in plastic wrap; freeze until firm.

coconut oatmeal biscotti
makes 18 biscotti

    1 cup QUAKER® Oats (quick or
        old fashioned, uncooked)
    1 cup flaked sweetened coconut
    ½ cup toasted chopped pecans
    1¾ cups all-purpose flour
    ¾ cup firmly packed brown sugar
    1½ teaspoons baking powder
    ½ teaspoon salt
    2 large eggs
    ¼ cup light coconut milk
    1 teaspoon vanilla
    ½ cup white chocolate chips

1. Preheat oven to 350°F. Line baking sheet with parchment paper. Set aside.

2. Combine oats, coconut and pecans in food processor; process until finely ground. Lightly spoon flour into dry measuring cups; level with knife. Combine oat mixture, flour, brown sugar, baking powder and salt in large bowl; mix well. Combine eggs, coconut milk and vanilla in small bowl; mix well. Add to dry ingredients all at once; stir just until dry ingredients are moistened.

3. Turn dough out onto floured surface; knead lightly seven times with floured hands. Shape dough into 15×3-inch log on prepared baking sheet; pat to 1-inch thickness.

4. Bake 30 minutes. Remove to wire rack to cool.

5. Cut roll diagonally into 18 (½-inch) slices. Place, cut sides down, on baking sheet. Reduce oven temperature to 325°F; bake 18 minutes. Turn cookies over; bake an additional 18 minutes. (Cookies will be slightly soft in center but will harden as they cool.) Remove to wire rack to cool completely.

6. Place white chocolate chips in small microwave-safe bowl; microwave on HIGH (100% power) 30 seconds or until almost melted, stirring until smooth. Spread evenly over tops of biscotti.

oatmeal-chip crispies
makes about 6 dozen cookies

    2 cups all-purpose flour
    1 teaspoon baking powder
    1 teaspoon baking soda
  ½ teaspoon salt
    1 cup (2 sticks) butter, softened
    1 cup packed brown sugar
  ¾ cup granulated sugar
    2 eggs
    1 teaspoon grated orange peel
    2 tablespoons orange juice
    2 cups old-fashioned oats
    1 cup dried cranberries
  ¾ cup white chocolate chips
  ¾ cup semisweet chocolate chips

1. Preheat oven to 350°F. Grease cookie sheets.

2. Combine flour, baking powder, baking soda and salt in medium bowl. Beat butter, brown sugar and granulated sugar in large bowl with electric mixer at medium speed 2 minutes. Add eggs, orange peel and orange juice; beat 1 minute. Add flour mixture; beat until well blended. Stir in oats, cranberries and chocolate chips until well blended.

3. Shape dough into 1-inch balls. Place 1½ inches apart on prepared cookie sheets. Flatten slightly to ⅜-inch thickness.

4. Bake 15 to 17 minutes or until lightly browned and firm to the touch. Cool cookies on cookie sheets 2 minutes; remove to wire racks to cool completely.

chocolate-dipped oat cookies
makes about 6 dozen cookies

2 cups old-fashioned oats
³⁄₄ cup packed brown sugar
¹⁄₂ cup finely chopped walnuts
¹⁄₂ cup vegetable oil
1 egg
2 teaspoons grated orange peel
¹⁄₄ teaspoon salt
1 package (12 ounces) milk chocolate chips

1. Combine oats, brown sugar, walnuts, oil, egg, orange peel and salt in large bowl until blended. Cover and refrigerate overnight.

2. Preheat oven to 350°F. Lightly grease cookie sheets or line with parchment paper. Shape oat mixture into large marble-sized balls. Place 2 inches apart on prepared cookie sheets.

3. Bake 10 to 12 minutes or until golden and crisp. Remove cookies to wire racks; cool 10 minutes.

4. Meanwhile, melt chocolate chips in microwave according to package directions. Dip tops of cookies, one at a time, into melted chocolate. Place on waxed paper; let stand until chocolate is set.

tip: When melting chocolate chips in the microwave, it's important to stir at 20- or 30-second intervals. The chocolate retains its original shape even when melted, so it may look like it needs more time when any additional cooking would actually scorch the chocolate.

double striped peanut butter oatmeal cookies

makes about 4 dozen cookies

- ¾ cup REESE'S® Creamy Peanut Butter
- ½ cup (1 stick) butter or margarine, softened
- ⅓ cup granulated sugar
- ⅓ cup packed light brown sugar
- 1 egg
- 2 tablespoons milk
- 1 teaspoon vanilla extract
- 1⅓ cups quick-cooking oats, divided
- 1 cup all-purpose flour
- 1 teaspoon baking soda
- ½ teaspoon salt
- ½ cup HERSHEY'S Milk Chocolate Chips
- 2 teaspoons shortening (do not use butter, margarine, spread or oil), divided
- ½ cup REESE'S® Peanut Butter Chips

1. Heat oven to 350°F. Beat peanut butter and butter in large bowl until well blended. Add granulated sugar and brown sugar; beat until fluffy. Add egg, milk and vanilla; beat well. Stir together ½ cup oats, flour, baking soda and salt; gradually beat into peanut butter mixture.

2. Shape dough into 1-inch balls. Roll in remaining oats; place on ungreased cookie sheet. Flatten cookies with tines of fork to form a crisscross pattern.

3. Bake 10 to 12 minutes or until lightly browned. Cool slightly; remove from cookie sheet to wire rack. Cool completely.

4. Place chocolate chips and 1 teaspoon shortening in medium microwave-safe container. Microwave at MEDIUM (50%) 30 seconds; stir. If necessary, microwave at MEDIUM an additional 10 seconds at a time, stirring after each heating, until chocolate is melted and smooth when stirred. Drizzle over cookies. Repeat procedure with peanut butter chips and remaining 1 teaspoon shortening. Allow drizzles to set.

maui waui cookies
makes about 3 dozen cookies

  2 cups all-purpose flour
  1 cup quick oats
½ teaspoon baking powder
½ teaspoon salt
½ teaspoon ground cinnamon
¼ teaspoon baking soda
  1 cup (2 sticks) unsalted butter, softened
  1 cup sugar
  1 egg
¾ cup coarsely chopped salted macadamia nuts
½ cup packed shredded coconut
    Pineapple Glaze (recipe follows)

1. Preheat oven to 400°F. Line two cookie sheets with parchment paper. Combine flour, oats, baking powder, salt, cinnamon and baking soda in medium bowl.

2. Beat butter and sugar in large bowl with electric mixer at medium-high speed. Beat in egg. Add flour mixture, ½ cup at a time, until well blended. Stir in macadamia nuts and coconut. Drop dough by 2 tablespoonfuls about 1½ inches apart onto prepared cookie sheets.

3. Bake 16 minutes or until cookies are set and edges are golden brown. Cool cookies on cookie sheets 2 minutes; remove parchment paper to wire racks to cool completely.

4. Prepare Pineapple Glaze; drizzle over cookies.

pineapple glaze: Place 1½ tablespoons melted butter in medium bowl. Stir in 1 cup powdered sugar and ⅛ teaspoon salt until blended. Add 4 to 5 teaspoons unsweetened pineapple juice, 1 teaspoon at a time, until glaze is consistency of thin pancake batter.

banana jumbles
makes 18 cookies

- **2 extra-ripe, medium DOLE® Bananas**
- **¾ cup packed brown sugar**
- **½ cup creamy peanut butter**
- **¼ cup margarine or butter, softened**
- **1 egg**
- **1½ cups old-fashioned oats**
- **1 cup all-purpose flour**
- **1½ teaspoons baking powder**
- **½ teaspoon salt**
- **¾ cup DOLE® Seedless Raisins**

• Mash bananas with fork. Measure 1 cup.

• Beat brown sugar, peanut butter and margarine in large bowl. Beat in egg and mashed bananas.

• Combine oats, flour, baking powder and salt. Stir into banana mixture until well combined. Stir in raisins.

• Drop by heaping tablespoonfuls onto cookie sheets coated with nonstick cooking spray. Shape cookies with back of spoon. Bake at 375°F 12 to 14 minutes or until lightly browned. Cool on wire racks.

carrot cake cookies
makes 28 cookies

    2 cups quick or old-fashioned oats
 1½ cups all-purpose flour
    1 teaspoon baking soda
    1 teaspoon salt
 1¼ cups firmly packed light brown sugar
    4 tablespoons PROMISE® Buttery Spread
    2 tablespoons Neufchâtel or ⅓ less fat cream cheese, softened
   ⅓ cup lowfat vanilla yogurt
    1 large egg
    1 teaspoon vanilla extract
    1 cup raisins
   ½ cup shredded carrot (about 1 large carrot)

Combine oats, flour, baking soda and salt in medium bowl; set aside.

Beat brown sugar, PROMISE® Buttery Spread and cream cheese in large bowl with electric mixer until creamy, about 3 minutes. Beat in yogurt, egg and vanilla until blended. Gradually beat in oat mixture just until blended. Stir in raisins and carrot.

Turn dough onto waxed paper and form into four 7-inch-long logs. Wrap tightly and freeze 2 hours or until firm.

Preheat oven to 375°F. For 2 servings, slice off four 1-inch rounds from log, then refreeze remaining dough until ready to bake. Arrange frozen cookie slices on baking sheet. Let stand 10 minutes. Bake 8 minutes or until edges are golden and centers are set. Cool 2 minutes on wire rack; remove from baking sheet and cool completely.

tip: Need more cookies? Slice, then bake as many as you need using the above directions.

prep time: 15 minutes • **freeze time:** 2 hours • **bake time:** 8 minutes

gingery oat & molasses cookies

makes about 4 dozen cookies

   1 cup all-purpose flour
 ¾ cup whole wheat flour
 ½ cup old-fashioned oats
1½ teaspoons baking powder
1½ teaspoons ground ginger
   1 teaspoon baking soda
 ½ teaspoon ground cinnamon
 ¼ teaspoon salt
 ¾ cup sugar
 ½ cup (1 stick) unsalted butter, softened
   1 egg
 ¼ cup molasses
 ¼ teaspoon vanilla
   1 cup chopped crystallized ginger
 ½ cup chopped walnuts

1. Combine all-purpose flour, whole wheat flour, oats, baking powder, ground ginger, baking soda, cinnamon and salt in medium bowl.

2. Beat sugar and butter in large bowl with electric mixer at high speed until light and fluffy. Beat in egg, molasses and vanilla. Gradually beat in flour mixture. Stir in crystallized ginger and walnuts. Shape into two logs 8 to 10 inches long. Wrap logs in plastic wrap; refrigerate 1 to 3 hours.

3. Preheat oven to 350°F. Grease cookie sheets. Cut logs into ⅓-inch slices; place 1½ inches apart on prepared cookie sheets.

4. Bake 12 to 14 minutes or until set. Cool cookies on cookie sheets 5 minutes; remove to wire racks to cool completely.

pumpkin-oatmeal raisin cookies

makes 4 dozen cookies

2 cups all-purpose flour
1⅓ cups quick or old-fashioned oats
2 teaspoons pumpkin pie spice
1 teaspoon baking soda
½ teaspoon salt
1 cup (2 sticks) butter or margarine, softened
1 cup packed brown sugar
1 cup granulated sugar
1 cup LIBBY'S® 100% Pure Pumpkin
1 large egg
1 teaspoon vanilla extract
¾ cup chopped walnuts
¾ cup raisins

PREHEAT oven to 350°F. Lightly grease baking sheets.

COMBINE flour, oats, pie spice, baking soda and salt in medium bowl. Beat butter, brown sugar and granulated sugar in large mixer bowl until light and fluffy. Add pumpkin, egg and vanilla extract; mix well. Add flour mixture; mix well. Stir in nuts and raisins. Drop by rounded tablespoons onto prepared baking sheets.

BAKE for 14 to 16 minutes or until cookies are lightly browned and set in centers. Cool on baking sheets for 2 minutes; remove to wire racks to cool completely.

white chocolate cranberry dippers
makes about 1½ dozen cookies

1 package (about 18 ounces) spice cake mix
1 cup old-fashioned oats
⅓ cup vegetable oil
2 eggs
1 teaspoon vanilla
2½ cups white chocolate chips, divided
1 cup dried cranberries
1 cup chopped walnuts or pecans (optional)
3 tablespoons shortening

1. Preheat oven to 350°F. Spray cookie sheets lightly with nonstick cooking spray.

2. Combine cake mix, oats, oil, eggs and vanilla in large bowl until well blended. Stir in 1 cup white chocolate chips, cranberries and walnuts, if desired. Drop dough by tablespoonfuls 2 inches apart onto prepared cookie sheets.

3. Bake 10 minutes or until edges are lightly browned. Cool cookies on cookie sheets 5 minutes; remove to wire racks to cool completely.

4. Place remaining 1½ cups white chocolate chips and shortening in small microwavable bowl; microwave on HIGH 15 seconds. Stir until mixture is melted and smooth. (Heat additional 10 seconds, if necessary.)

5. Spread sheet of waxed paper on work surface. Dip each cookie into chocolate mixture and allow excess to drip into bowl. Place cookies on waxed paper until chocolate is set.

chewy chocolate no-bakes
makes about 36 treats

1 cup (6 ounces) semisweet chocolate chips
5 tablespoons light butter
14 large marshmallows
1 teaspoon vanilla
2 cups QUAKER® Oats (quick or old fashioned, uncooked)
²⁄₃ cup (any combination of) raisins, diced dried mixed fruit, shredded coconut, miniature marshmallows or chopped nuts

1. Melt chocolate chips, butter and large marshmallows in large saucepan over low heat, stirring until smooth. Remove from heat; cool slightly. Stir in vanilla. Stir in oats and remaining ingredients.

2. Drop by rounded tablespoonfuls onto waxed paper. Cover and refrigerate 2 to 3 hours. Let stand at room temperature about 15 minutes before serving. Store, tightly covered, in refrigerator.

microwave directions: Place chocolate chips, butter and marshmallows in large microwave-safe bowl. Microwave on HIGH (100% power) 1 to 2 minutes or until mixture is melted and smooth, stirring every 30 seconds. Proceed as directed.

pb & j thumbprint cookies

makes about 3½ dozen cookies

    2 cups old-fashioned oats
 1⅓ cups plus 1 tablespoon all-purpose flour
   ¾ teaspoon baking soda
   ½ teaspoon baking powder
   ½ teaspoon salt
    1 cup packed brown sugar
   ¾ cup (1½ sticks) butter, softened
   ¼ cup granulated sugar
   ¼ cup chunky peanut butter
    1 egg
    1 tablespoon honey
    1 teaspoon vanilla
   ½ cup chopped peanuts, unsalted or honey-roasted
   ½ cup grape jelly or favorite flavor

1. Preheat oven to 350°F. Line cookie sheets with parchment paper.

2. Combine oats, flour, baking soda, baking powder and salt in medium bowl. Beat brown sugar, butter and granulated sugar in large bowl with electric mixer at medium speed until well blended. Beat at high speed until light and fluffy.

3. Add peanut butter, egg, honey and vanilla; beat at medium speed until well blended. Gradually add flour mixture; beat just until blended. Stir in peanuts. Drop dough by rounded tablespoonfuls onto prepared cookie sheets.

4. Bake 10 minutes. Press center of each cookie with back of teaspoon to make a slight indentation; fill with about ½ teaspoon jelly. Bake 4 to 6 minutes or until puffed and golden. Cool cookies on cookie sheets 5 minutes; remove to wire racks to cool completely.

chewy fruit and oatmeal cookies

makes 36 cookies

¾ **cup firmly packed brown sugar**
½ **cup granulated sugar**
1 **container (8 ounces) low-fat vanilla or plain yogurt**
2 **large egg whites, lightly beaten**
2 **tablespoons vegetable oil**
2 **tablespoons fat-free (skim) milk**
2 **teaspoons vanilla**
1½ **cups all-purpose flour**
1 **teaspoon baking soda**
1 **teaspoon ground cinnamon**
½ **teaspoon salt (optional)**
3 **cups QUAKER® Oats (quick or old fashioned, uncooked)**
1 **cup diced dried mixed fruit, raisins or dried cranberries**

1. Heat oven to 350°F. Combine sugars, yogurt, egg whites, oil, milk and vanilla in large bowl; mix well. Combine flour, baking soda, cinnamon and salt, if desired, in medium bowl; mix well. Add to yogurt mixture; mix well. Stir in oats and dried fruit.

2. Drop dough by rounded tablespoonfuls onto ungreased cookie sheets.

3. Bake 12 to 14 minutes or until light golden brown. Cool 1 minute on cookie sheets; remove to wire racks. Cool completely. Store loosely covered.

double chocolate coconut oatmeal cookies

makes about 2½ dozen cookies

- 1¾ **cups packed light brown sugar**
- 1 **cup shortening**
- 3 **eggs**
- 2 **teaspoons vanilla extract**
- 1⅓ **cups all-purpose flour**
- ½ **cup HERSHEY'S Cocoa**
- 2 **teaspoons baking soda**
- ¼ **teaspoon salt**
- ½ **cup water**
- 3 **cups rolled oats or quick-cooking oats**
- 2 **cups (12-ounce package) HERSHEY'S SPECIAL DARK Chocolate Chips or HERSHEY'S Semi-Sweet Chocolate Chips, divided**
- 2 **cups MOUNDS® Sweetened Coconut Flakes, divided**
- 1 **cup coarsely chopped nuts**

1. Beat brown sugar, shortening, eggs and vanilla in large bowl until well blended. Stir together flour, cocoa, baking soda and salt; add alternately with water to shortening mixture. Stir in oats, 1 cup chocolate chips, 1 cup coconut and nuts, blending well. Cover; refrigerate 2 hours.

2. Heat oven to 350°F. Lightly grease cookie sheet or line with parchment paper. Using ¼-cup ice cream scoop or measuring cup, drop dough about 4 inches apart onto prepared cookie sheet. Sprinkle cookie tops with remaining coconut. Top with remaining chocolate chips (about 9 chips per cookie); lightly press into dough.

3. Bake 10 to 12 minutes or until set (do not overbake). Cool slightly; remove from cookie sheet to wire rack. Cool completely.

oat, chocolate and hazelnut biscotti

makes about 4 dozen biscotti

1½ **cups whole wheat flour**
1 **cup all-purpose flour**
1 **cup old-fashioned oats**
2 **teaspoons baking powder**
½ **teaspoon salt**
½ **teaspoon ground cinnamon**
1½ **cups sugar**
½ **cup (1 stick) butter, softened**
3 **eggs**
1 **teaspoon vanilla**
2 **cups toasted hazelnuts (see Tip)**
¾ **cup semisweet chocolate chunks**

1. Preheat oven to 325°F. Line cookie sheet with parchment paper. Combine whole wheat flour, all-purpose flour, oats, baking powder, salt and cinnamon in large bowl.

2. Beat sugar and butter in large bowl with electric mixer at high speed until light and fluffy. Beat in eggs and vanilla. Gradually beat in flour mixture at low speed. Stir in hazelnuts and chocolate.

3. Divide dough in half. Shape each half into 10- to 12-inch log; flatten slightly to 3-inch width. Place on prepared cookie sheet.

4. Bake 30 minutes. Cool completely on cookie sheet. *Reduce oven temperature to 300°F.* Transfer logs to cutting board; cut diagonally into ½-inch slices with serrated knife. Arrange slices, cut side up, on cookie sheet.

5. Bake 10 to 15 minutes or until golden brown. Turn slices; bake 5 to 10 minutes or until golden brown. Remove to wire racks to cool completely.

tip: To toast hazelnuts, preheat oven to 325°F. Spread hazelnuts on a baking sheet; bake 5 to 7 minutes. Place nuts in a clean kitchen towel and rub to remove skins.

oatmeal candied chippers
makes about 4 dozen cookies

- ¾ **cup (1½ sticks) butter, softened**
- ¾ **cup granulated sugar**
- ¾ **cup packed light brown sugar**
- 3 **tablespoons milk**
- 1 **egg**
- 2 **teaspoons vanilla**
- ¾ **cup all-purpose flour**
- ¾ **teaspoon salt**
- ½ **teaspoon baking soda**
- 3 **cups old-fashioned or quick oats**
- 1⅓ **cups (10-ounce package) candy-coated chocolate pieces**

1. Preheat oven to 375°F. Grease cookie sheets.

2. Beat butter, granulated sugar and brown sugar in large bowl with electric mixer until light and fluffy. Add milk, egg and vanilla; beat until well blended. Add flour, salt and baking soda; beat until blended. Stir in oats and chocolate pieces. Drop dough by rounded tablespoonfuls 2 inches apart onto prepared cookie sheets.

3. Bake 10 to 12 minutes or until edges are golden brown. Cool cookies on cookie sheets 2 minutes; remove to wire racks to cool completely.

tip: Leaving butter out at room temperature an hour or 2 before baking is a good way soften it. If you need the butter more quickly, microwave it on LOW (30%) for 5-second intervals, turning occasionally, until it softens.

chocolate chip cherry oatmeal cookies

makes about 4 dozen cookies

⅔ cup sugar
⅓ cup canola oil
1 egg
1 teaspoon vanilla
¾ cup all-purpose flour
½ teaspoon baking soda
½ teaspoon ground cinnamon
⅛ teaspoon salt
1½ cups quick oats
½ cup dried cherries, raisins or cranberries
¼ cup mini semisweet chocolate chips

1. Preheat oven to 325°F. Spray cookie sheets with nonstick cooking spray.

2. Beat sugar, oil, egg and vanilla in large bowl with electric mixer at medium speed until well blended. Add flour, baking soda, cinnamon and salt; beat until blended. Stir in oats, cherries and chocolate chips.

3. Drop dough by slightly rounded teaspoonfuls about 2 inches apart onto prepared cookie sheets.

4. Bake 7 minutes (cookies will not brown). Cool cookies on cookie sheets 2 minutes; remove to wire racks to cool completely.

milk chocolate florentine cookies

makes about 3½ dozen sandwich cookies

- ⅔ **cup butter**
- 2 **cups quick oats**
- 1 **cup granulated sugar**
- ⅔ **cup all-purpose flour**
- ¼ **cup light or dark corn syrup**
- ¼ **cup milk**
- 1 **teaspoon vanilla extract**
- ¼ **teaspoon salt**
- 1¾ **cups (11.5-ounce package) NESTLÉ® TOLL HOUSE® Milk Chocolate Morsels**

PREHEAT oven to 375°F. Line baking sheets with foil.

MELT butter in medium saucepan; remove from heat. Stir in oats, sugar, flour, corn syrup, milk, vanilla extract and salt; mix well. Drop by level teaspoon, about 3 inches apart, onto prepared baking sheets. Spread thinly with rubber spatula.

BAKE for 6 to 8 minutes or until golden brown. Cool completely on baking sheets on wire racks. Peel foil from cookies.

MICROWAVE morsels in medium, uncovered, microwave-safe bowl on MEDIUM-HIGH (70%) power for 1 minute. Stir. Morsels may retain some of their original shape. If necessary, microwave at additional 10- to 15-second intervals, stirring just until morsels are melted. Spread thin layer of melted chocolate onto flat side of *half* the cookies. Top with *remaining* cookies.

whole grain chippers
makes about 6 dozen cookies

  1 cup (2 sticks) butter, softened
  1 cup packed light brown sugar
  ²/₃ cup granulated sugar
  2 eggs
  1 teaspoon baking soda
  1 teaspoon vanilla
    Pinch salt
  2 cups old-fashioned oats
  1 cup all-purpose flour
  1 cup whole wheat flour
  1 package (12 ounces) semisweet chocolate chips
  1 cup sunflower seeds

1. Preheat oven to 375°F. Lightly grease cookie sheets or line with parchment paper.

2. Beat butter, brown sugar, granulated sugar and eggs in large bowl with electric mixer at medium speed until light and fluffy. Beat in baking soda, vanilla and salt. Blend in oats, all-purpose flour and whole wheat flour to make stiff dough. Stir in chocolate chips.

3. Shape rounded teaspoonfuls of dough into balls; roll in sunflower seeds. Place 2 inches apart on prepared cookie sheets.

4. Bake 8 to 10 minutes or until firm. *Do not overbake.* Cool cookies on cookie sheets 2 minutes; remove to wire racks to cool completely.

oatmeal gingerbread cookies
makes 20 (5-inch) cookies

1 cup (2 sticks) margarine or butter, softened
3/4 cup firmly packed brown sugar
1/2 cup molasses
1 egg
3 1/3 cups all-purpose flour
1 1/2 cups QUAKER® Oats (quick or old fashioned, uncooked)
1 teaspoon ground cinnamon
1 teaspoon ground ginger
1/2 teaspoon ground nutmeg
1/2 teaspoon baking soda
1/4 teaspoon salt (optional)
Ready-to-spread frosting
Assorted candies

1. Beat margarine and brown sugar in large bowl until creamy. Add molasses and egg; beat well. Add combined flour, oats, cinnamon, ginger, nutmeg, baking soda and salt, if desired; mix well. Cover; chill about 2 hours.

2. Heat oven to 350°F. On floured surface, roll dough out about 1/4 inch thick for a chewy cookie or 1/8 inch thick for a crisp cookie. Cut with 5-inch gingerbread man or woman cookie cutter. Place on ungreased cookie sheets.

3. Bake 8 to 10 minutes or until set. Cool 1 minute on cookie sheets; remove to wire racks. Cool completely.

4. Frost and decorate cookies with candies. Store loosely covered at room temperature.

blue-ribbon bars

chocolate and oat toffee bars
makes 2½ dozen bars

- ¾ cup (1½ sticks) plus 2 tablespoons butter, softened, divided
- 1 package (about 18 ounces) yellow cake mix with pudding in the mix
- 2 cups quick oats
- ¼ cup packed brown sugar
- 1 egg
- ½ teaspoon vanilla
- 1 cup toffee baking bits
- ½ cup chopped pecans
- ⅓ cup semisweet chocolate chips

1. Preheat oven to 350°F. Grease 13×9-inch baking pan.

2. Beat ¾ cup butter in large bowl with electric mixer at medium speed until creamy. Add cake mix, oats, brown sugar, egg and vanilla; beat 1 minute or until well blended. Stir in toffee bits and pecans. Pat dough into prepared pan.

3. Bake 30 to 35 minutes or until golden brown. Cool completely in pan on wire rack.

4. Melt remaining 2 tablespoons butter and chocolate chips in small saucepan over low heat. Drizzle warm glaze over bars. Let stand at room temperature 1 hour or until glaze is set.

cinnamon apple pie bars
makes about 2 dozen bars

1 package (about 18 ounces) spice cake mix with pudding in the mix
2 cups old-fashioned oats
½ teaspoon ground cinnamon
¾ cup (1½ sticks) butter, cut into pieces
1 egg
1 can (21 ounces) apple pie filling

1. Preheat oven to 350°F. Spray 13×9-inch baking pan with nonstick cooking spray.

2. Combine cake mix, oats and cinnamon in large bowl. Cut in butter with pastry blender or two knives until butter is evenly distributed and no large pieces remain (mixture will be dry and have clumps). Stir in egg until well blended.

3. Press about three fourths of oat mixture evenly into bottom of prepared pan. Spread apple pie filling evenly over top. Crumble remaining oat mixture over filling.

4. Bake 25 to 30 minutes or until top and edges are lightly browned. Cool completely in pan on wire rack. Cut into bars.

ooey-gooey caramel peanut butter bars
makes about 2 dozen bars

1 package (about 18 ounces) yellow cake mix *without* pudding in the mix
1 cup quick oats
²/₃ cup creamy peanut butter
1 egg, slightly beaten
2 tablespoons milk
1 package (8 ounces) cream cheese, softened
1 jar (12¼ ounces) caramel ice cream topping
1 cup semisweet chocolate chips

1. Preheat oven to 350°F. Lightly grease 13×9-inch baking pan.

2. Combine cake mix and oats in large bowl. Cut in peanut butter with pastry blender or two knives until mixture is crumbly.

3. Blend egg and milk in small bowl. Add to peanut butter mixture; stir just until combined. Reserve 1½ cups mixture. Press remaining peanut butter mixture into prepared pan.

4. Beat cream cheese in medium bowl with electric mixer at medium speed until fluffy. Add caramel topping; beat just until combined. Carefully spread over peanut butter layer in pan. Break up reserved peanut butter mixture into small pieces; sprinkle over cream cheese layer. Sprinkle with chocolate chips.

5. Bake 30 minutes or until nearly set in center. Cool completely in pan on wire rack.

spirited southern sweet potato bars

makes 32 bars

    2 cups QUAKER® Oats (quick or
        old fashioned, uncooked)
 1½ cups all-purpose flour
   ¼ teaspoon salt (optional)
   ⅛ to ¼ teaspoon ground red pepper
    1 cup (2 sticks) butter or margarine,
        softened
   ⅔ cup granulated sugar
    1 teaspoon vanilla
    2 cups mashed cooked sweet potato or canned pumpkin
   ¾ cup firmly packed brown sugar
    2 eggs, lightly beaten
    2 tablespoons bourbon or ½ teaspoon rum extract (optional)
    1 cup chopped pecans

1. Heat oven to 375°F. Lightly grease 13×9-inch baking pan.

2. Combine oats and flour in large bowl; mix well. Measure ⅔ cup of mixture into small bowl; stir in salt, if desired, and red pepper. Set aside.

3. Add butter, granulated sugar and vanilla to remaining oat mixture; blend with electric mixer on low to medium speed until crumbly. Reserve 1 cup for topping. Press remaining mixture evenly onto bottom of prepared pan. Bake 15 minutes; remove pan from oven.

4. Combine sweet potato, brown sugar, reserved ⅔ cup oat mixture, eggs and bourbon, if desired, in separate bowl; mix well. Spread filling over warm crust. Add pecans to reserved topping mixture; mix well. Sprinkle evenly over sweet potato filling.

5. Bake 30 to 35 minutes or until topping is light golden brown. Cool in pan on wire rack; cut into bars. Serve at room temperature. Store in refrigerator tightly covered.

premier cheesecake cranberry bars

makes 2½ dozen bars

- 2 cups all-purpose flour
- 1½ cups quick or old-fashioned oats
- ¼ cup packed light brown sugar
- 1 cup (2 sticks) butter or margarine, softened
- 2 cups (12-ounce package) NESTLÉ® TOLL HOUSE® Premier White Morsels
- 1 package (8 ounces) cream cheese, softened
- 1 can (14 ounces) NESTLÉ® CARNATION® Sweetened Condensed Milk
- ¼ cup lemon juice
- 1 teaspoon vanilla extract
- 1 can (14 ounces) whole-berry cranberry sauce
- 2 tablespoons cornstarch

PREHEAT oven to 350°F. Grease 13×9-inch baking pan.

COMBINE flour, oats and brown sugar in large bowl. Add butter; mix until crumbly. Stir in morsels. Reserve *2½ cups* morsel mixture for topping. With floured fingers, press *remaining* mixture into prepared pan.

BEAT cream cheese in large mixer bowl until creamy. Add sweetened condensed milk, lemon juice and vanilla extract; mix until smooth. Pour over crust. Combine cranberry sauce and cornstarch in medium bowl. Spoon over cream cheese mixture. Sprinkle *reserved* morsel mixture over cranberry mixture.

BAKE for 35 to 40 minutes or until center is set. Cool completely in pan on wire rack. Cover; refrigerate until serving time (up to 1 day). Cut into bars.

chocolate chunk oat bars
makes 16 bars

  1 cup all-purpose flour
  ½ teaspoon baking soda
  ½ teaspoon salt
  1 cup packed light brown sugar
  ½ cup (1 stick) butter, softened
  1 egg
  1 tablespoon water
  1 teaspoon vanilla
1½ cups old-fashioned oats
  2 cups semisweet chocolate chunks, divided

1. Preheat oven to 375°F. Lightly grease 9-inch square baking pan. Combine flour, baking soda and salt in small bowl.

2. Beat brown sugar and butter in large bowl with electric mixer at medium-high speed until creamy. Add egg, water and vanilla; beat until well blended. Stir in flour mixture and oats; mix well. Stir in 1½ cups chocolate chunks.

3. Spread dough evenly in prepared pan; sprinkle with remaining ½ cup chocolate chunks.

4. Bake about 30 minutes or just until center feels firm. Cool completely in pan on wire rack.

apricot oatmeal bars
makes 16 bars

    1½ cups old-fashioned oats
    1¼ cups all-purpose flour
    ½ cup packed light brown sugar
     1 teaspoon ground ginger, divided
    ½ teaspoon baking soda
    ½ teaspoon salt
    ½ teaspoon cinnamon
    ¾ cup (1½ sticks) butter, melted
    1¼ cups apricot preserves

1. Preheat oven to 350°F. Line 8-inch square baking pan with foil.

2. Combine oats, flour, brown sugar, ½ teaspoon ginger, baking soda, salt and cinnamon in large bowl. Add butter; stir just until moistened and crumbly. Reserve 1½ cups oat mixture. Press remaining oat mixture evenly onto bottom of prepared pan.

3. Combine preserves and remaining ½ teaspoon ginger in small bowl. Spread preserves mixture evenly over crust. Sprinkle with reserved oat mixture.

4. Bake 30 minutes or until golden brown. Cool completely in pan on wire rack. Cut into bars.

peanut butter cereal bars
makes 2 dozen bars

   3 cups mini marshmallows
   3 tablespoons butter
   ½ cup peanut butter
 3½ cups crisp rice cereal
   1 cup quick oats
   ⅓ cup mini semisweet chocolate chips

microwave directions

1. Lightly spray 13×9-inch baking pan with nonstick cooking spray.

2. Combine marshmallows and butter in large microwavable bowl. Microwave on HIGH 15 seconds; stir. Microwave 1 minute; stir until marshmallows are melted and mixture is smooth. Stir in peanut butter. Add cereal and oats; stir until well coated.

3. Spread mixture in prepared pan. Immediately sprinkle with chocolate chips; lightly press chips into cereal. Cool completely before cutting into bars.

> tip: To make spreading the cereal mixture easier and make cleanup a snap, lightly spray your spoon with nonstick cooking spray before stirring the marshmallow mixture.

oatmeal date bars

makes about 2 dozen bars

2 packages (about 16 ounces each) refrigerated oatmeal raisin cookie dough, divided
2½ cups old-fashioned oats, divided
2 packages (8 ounces each) chopped dates
1 cup water
½ cup sugar
1 teaspoon vanilla

1. Let dough stand at room temperature 15 minutes. Preheat oven to 350°F. Lightly grease 13×9-inch baking pan.

2. For topping, combine ¾ package dough and 1 cup oats in medium bowl; beat until well blended.

3. For crust, combine remaining 1¼ packages dough and remaining 1½ cups oats in large bowl; beat until well blended. Press dough evenly onto bottom of prepared pan. Bake 10 minutes.

4. Meanwhile, for filling, combine dates, water and sugar in medium saucepan; bring to a boil over high heat. Boil 3 minutes; remove from heat and stir in vanilla. Spread date mixture evenly over partially baked crust; sprinkle with topping mixture.

5. Bake 25 to 28 minutes or until bubbly. Cool completely in pan on wire rack.

triple peanut butter oatmeal bars
makes 32 bars

    1½ cups firmly packed brown sugar
     1 cup peanut butter
    ½ cup (1 stick) margarine or butter, softened
     2 large eggs
     1 teaspoon vanilla
     2 cups QUAKER® Oats (quick or old fashioned, uncooked)
     1 cup all-purpose flour
    ½ teaspoon baking soda
     1 bag (8 ounces) candy-coated peanut butter pieces
    ½ cup chopped peanuts

1. Heat oven to 350°F. Lightly spray 13×9-inch baking pan with nonstick cooking spray.

2. Beat brown sugar, peanut butter and margarine in large bowl with electric mixer until creamy. Add eggs and vanilla; beat well. Add combined oats, flour and baking soda; mix well. Stir in peanut butter pieces. Spread dough evenly into pan. Sprinkle with peanuts, pressing in lightly with fingers.

3. Bake 35 to 40 minutes or just until center is set. Cool completely on wire rack. Cut into bars. Store tightly covered.

banana oatmeal snack bars

makes 2 dozen bars

2 packages (about 16 ounces each)
    refrigerated oatmeal raisin
    cookie dough
2 bananas, mashed
3 eggs
½ teaspoon ground cinnamon
1 cup old-fashioned oats
1 cup dried cranberries
½ cup chopped dried apricots
½ cup chopped pecans
    Powdered sugar

1. Let dough stand at room temperature 15 minutes. Preheat oven to 350°F. Lightly grease 13×9-inch baking pan.

2. Beat dough, bananas, eggs and cinnamon in large bowl until well blended. Combine oats, cranberries, apricots and pecans in medium bowl. Stir oat mixture into dough mixture until well blended. Spread evenly in prepared pan.

3. Bake 40 to 45 minutes or until top is browned and center is firm to the touch. Cool completely in pan on wire rack. Cut into bars. Sprinkle with powdered sugar.

cobbled fruit bars

makes about 3 dozen bars

1½ cups apple juice
1 cup chopped dried apricots
1 cup raisins
1 package (6 ounces) dried cherries
1 teaspoon cornstarch
1 teaspoon ground cinnamon
1 package (about 18 ounces) yellow
    cake mix
2 cups old-fashioned oats
¾ cup (1½ sticks) butter, melted
1 egg

1. Combine apple juice, apricots, raisins, cherries, cornstarch and cinnamon in medium saucepan, stirring until cornstarch is dissolved. Bring to a boil; cook 5 minutes, stirring constantly. Remove from heat; cool to room temperature.

2. Preheat oven to 350°F. Line 15×10-inch jelly-roll pan with foil; spray lightly with nonstick cooking spray.

3. Combine cake mix and oats in large bowl; stir in butter. Add egg; stir until well blended. Press three fourths of dough into prepared pan. Spread fruit mixture evenly over top. Sprinkle with remaining dough.

4. Bake 25 to 30 minutes or until edges and top are lightly browned. Cool completely in pan on wire rack.

buttery oatmeal turtle bars
makes 3 to 4 dozen bars

    1 cup all-purpose flour
    1 cup old-fashioned oats
    ¾ cup plus ⅔ cup packed brown sugar, divided
    1 cup (2 sticks) butter, softened, divided
    1½ cups pecans
    ½ teaspoon vanilla
    4 ounces semisweet or milk chocolate, broken into 1-inch chunks

1. Preheat oven to 350°F. Combine flour, oats, ¾ cup brown sugar and ½ cup butter in medium bowl until well blended. Pat firmly into ungreased 13×9-inch baking pan. Sprinkle with pecans.

2. For topping, combine remaining ⅔ cup brown sugar and ½ cup butter in small saucepan. Cook over medium heat, stirring constantly, until mixture comes to a rolling boil. Boil 1 minute. Remove from heat; stir in vanilla. Pour evenly over crust.

3. Bake 15 to 18 minutes or until caramel is bubbly.

4. Sprinkle chocolate evenly over caramel layer. Bake 1 minute to melt chocolate, then swirl chocolate to marble. Cool slightly; refrigerate until set. Cut into bars.

> **tip:** To soften brown sugar that has hardened, place it in a microwavable bowl and cover with plastic wrap. Microwave on HIGH 30 to 45 seconds; stir and repeat, if necessary. Keep a close watch on the sugar so it doesn't melt.

berry berry streusel bars
makes 16 bars

- 1½ cups QUAKER® Oats (quick or old fashioned, uncooked)
- 1¼ cups all-purpose flour
- ¾ cup (1½ sticks) butter or margarine, melted
- ½ cup firmly packed brown sugar
- 1 cup fresh or frozen blueberries (do not thaw)
- ⅓ cup raspberry or strawberry preserves
- 1 teaspoon all-purpose flour
- ½ teaspoon grated lemon peel (optional)

1. Heat oven to 350°F. Combine oats, flour, butter and brown sugar; mix until crumbly. Reserve 1 cup oat mixture for topping. Set aside. Press remaining mixture onto bottom of ungreased 8- or 9-inch square baking pan. Bake 13 to 15 minutes or until light golden brown. Cool slightly.

2. Combine blueberries, preserves, flour and lemon peel, if desired, in medium bowl; mix gently. Spread over crust. Sprinkle with reserved oat mixture, patting gently.

3. Bake 20 to 22 minutes or until light golden brown. Cool completely. Cut into bars. Store tightly covered.

oat-y nut bars
makes 16 bars

- **½ cup (1 stick) butter**
- **½ cup honey**
- **¼ cup packed brown sugar**
- **¼ cup corn syrup**
- **2¾ cups quick oats**
- **⅔ cup raisins**
- **½ cup salted peanuts**

1. Preheat oven to 300°F. Grease 9-inch square baking pan.

2. Heat butter, honey, brown sugar and corn syrup in medium saucepan over medium heat, stirring constantly. Bring to a boil; boil 8 minutes or until mixture thickens slightly.

3. Stir in oats, raisins and peanuts until well blended. Press evenly into prepared pan.

4. Bake 25 to 30 minutes or until golden brown. Score into 2-inch squares. Cool completely in pan on wire rack. Cut into bars along score lines.

tip: Quick oats and old-fashioned oats are essentially the same; the quick oats simply cook faster because they have been cut into pieces and rolled into thinner flakes. They are interchangeable in many recipes.

chocolate oatmeal caramel bars

makes 16 bars

- 1¼ cups old-fashioned oats
- 1 cup all-purpose flour
- ½ cup plus 2 tablespoons packed brown sugar, divided
- 2 tablespoons unsweetened Dutch process cocoa powder*
- ¾ cup (1½ sticks) butter, melted
- 1 can (14 ounces) sweetened condensed milk
- ⅓ cup butter
- ½ cup chopped pecans

*Unsweetened cocoa powder may be substituted. Dutch process cocoa powder has a stronger flavor and will bake a darker color.

1. Preheat oven to 350°F. Combine oats, flour, ½ cup brown sugar and cocoa in medium bowl. Add ¾ cup melted butter; mix until crumbly.

2. Reserve 1 cup oat mixture for topping; press remaining mixture into bottom of ungreased 8-inch square baking pan. Bake 15 minutes.

3. Combine condensed milk, ⅓ cup butter and remaining 2 tablespoons brown sugar in medium saucepan; cook and stir over medium heat about 10 minutes or until thick and pale brown in color.

4. Cool milk mixture slightly until thickened; spread evenly over baked crust. Let stand 5 minutes or until set. Add pecans to reserved oat mixture; sprinkle over caramel layer, patting down gently.

5. Bake 20 to 22 minutes or until golden brown. Cool completely in pan on wire rack. Cut into bars.

oatmeal & cranberry brownie bars

makes 32 bars

2½ **cups quick or old-fashioned oats**
¾ **cup all-purpose flour**
¾ **cup dried cranberries, coarsely chopped**
½ **teaspoon baking soda**
¾ **cup (1½ sticks) butter, softened**
½ **cup packed brown sugar**
4 **eggs, divided**
1 **teaspoon vanilla**
1 **package (19½ ounces) traditional fudge brownie mix**
½ **cup vegetable oil**
¼ **cup water**
¾ **cup walnuts, coarsely chopped**

1. Preheat oven to 350°F. Lightly spray 13×9-inch baking pan with nonstick cooking spray.

2. Combine oats, flour, cranberries and baking soda in medium bowl. Beat butter and brown sugar in large bowl with electric mixer at medium speed until creamy. Add 2 eggs and vanilla; beat until well blended. Add oat mixture; beat just until blended. Press dough evenly into prepared pan.

3. Combine brownie mix, oil, water and remaining 2 eggs in large bowl; mix just until combined. Stir in walnuts. Spread brownie batter over oatmeal base.

4. Bake 35 to 38 minutes or until toothpick inserted into center comes out clean. Cool completely on wire rack. Cut into bars. Store in airtight container.

o'henrietta bars
makes 24 bars

Cooking spray
½ cup (1 stick) butter or margarine, softened
½ cup packed brown sugar
½ cup KARO® Light or Dark Corn Syrup
1 teaspoon vanilla
3 cups quick oats, uncooked
½ cup (3 ounces) semisweet chocolate chips
¼ cup creamy peanut butter

1. Preheat oven to 350°F. Spray 8- or 9-inch square baking pan with cooking spray.

2. Beat butter, brown sugar, corn syrup and vanilla in large bowl with mixer at medium speed until smooth. Stir in oats. Press into prepared pan.

3. Bake 25 minutes or until center is barely firm. Cool on wire rack 5 minutes.

4. Sprinkle with chocolate chips; top with small spoonfuls of peanut butter. Let stand 5 minutes; spread peanut butter and chocolate over bars, swirling to marble.

5. Cool completely on wire rack before cutting. Cut into bars; refrigerate 15 minutes to set topping.

prep time: 20 minutes • **bake time:** 25 minutes, plus cooling

gingery cranberry apple crisp
makes 9 servings

    1 cup old-fashioned oats
 ¾ cup all-purpose flour
 ½ cup packed brown sugar
    2 teaspoons finely chopped crystallized ginger
 ½ teaspoon ground cinnamon
 ¼ teaspoon salt
    6 tablespoons (¾ stick) butter, cut into small pieces
    1 can (16 ounces) whole berry cranberry sauce
    2 tablespoons cornstarch
    5 cups peeled and thinly sliced apples (about 5 medium)
       Whipped cream or ice cream (optional)

1. Preheat oven to 375°F.

2. Combine oats, flour, brown sugar, crystallized ginger, cinnamon and salt in medium bowl. Cut in butter with pastry blender or two knives until mixture resembles coarse crumbs.

3. Combine cranberry sauce and cornstarch in large saucepan; mix well. Heat over medium-high heat 2 minutes or until sauce bubbles, stirring occasionally. Add apples, tossing to coat. Spread into 8-inch square baking dish. Sprinkle oat mixture over fruit.

4. Bake 25 to 35 minutes or until apples are tender. Serve warm with whipped cream or ice cream, if desired.

chocolate-peanut butter oatmeal snacking cake

makes about 16 servings

1¼ cups boiling water
1 cup old-fashioned oats
1 cup granulated sugar
1 cup packed brown sugar
½ cup (1 stick) butter, softened
2 eggs, beaten
1 teaspoon vanilla
1¾ cups all-purpose flour
¼ cup unsweetened cocoa powder
1 teaspoon baking soda
1 cup (6 ounces) semisweet chocolate chips
1 package (12 ounces) chocolate and peanut butter chips

1. Preheat oven to 350°F. Grease 13×9-inch baking pan.

2. Combine boiling water and oats in large bowl; let stand 10 minutes. Stir until water is absorbed. Add granulated sugar, brown sugar and butter; beat with electric mixer at low speed 1 minute or until well blended. Beat in eggs and vanilla until blended.

3. Combine flour, cocoa and baking soda in medium bowl. Gradually beat into oat mixture until well blended. Stir in 1 cup chocolate chips. Pour into prepared pan. Sprinkle with chocolate and peanut butter chips.

4. Bake 40 minutes or until toothpick inserted into center comes out clean. Cool completely in pan on wire rack.

oatmeal brûlée with raspberry sauce
makes 4 servings

- 4¼ **cups water, divided**
- ½ **teaspoon salt**
- 3 **cups old-fashioned oats**
- 1 **cup whipping cream**
- ½ **teaspoon vanilla**
- ¾ **cup granulated sugar, divided**
- 3 **egg yolks**
- 6 **ounces frozen sweetened raspberries**
- 1 **teaspoon orange extract**
- 3 **tablespoons packed brown sugar**

1. Preheat oven to 300°F. Line baking sheet with foil. Bring 4 cups water and salt to a boil in medium saucepan. Add oats; cook over low heat 3 to 5 minutes or until water is absorbed and oats are tender, stirring occasionally.

2. Divide oatmeal among four large ramekins or ovenproof bowls. Place on prepared baking sheet.

3. Bring cream to a simmer in separate medium saucepan over medium heat. *Do not boil.* Remove from heat; stir in vanilla. Whisk ¼ cup granulated sugar and egg yolks in small bowl. Pour about ½ cup hot cream in thin stream into egg mixture, stirring constantly. Stir egg mixture back into saucepan with cream, whisking until well blended. Pour cream mixture evenly over oatmeal in ramekins.

4. Bake 35 minutes or until nearly set. Meanwhile, place raspberries, remaining ½ cup granulated sugar, ¼ cup water and orange extract in blender or food processor; blend until smooth. Pour sauce through strainer to remove seeds; discard seeds. Remove ramekins from oven; preheat broiler.

5. Sprinkle 1½ teaspoons brown sugar evenly over each serving. Broil 3 to 5 minutes or until tops are caramelized. Cool 5 to 10 minutes before serving. Serve with raspberry sauce.

apple cinnamon rice crisp
makes 8 servings

1 cup MINUTE® White or Brown Rice, uncooked
Nonstick cooking spray
1 can (20 ounces) apple pie filling
1 cup packed brown sugar, divided
½ cup raisins
½ cup walnuts, chopped
1 teaspoon ground cinnamon
1½ cups uncooked rolled oats
4 tablespoons margarine
Vanilla ice cream (optional)

Prepare rice according to package directions.

Preheat oven to 350°F. Spray 2-quart baking dish with nonstick cooking spray.

Combine rice, pie filling, ½ cup brown sugar, raisins, walnuts and cinnamon in medium bowl. Pour into prepared dish.

Combine remaining ½ cup brown sugar and rolled oats in same bowl. Cut in margarine with pastry blender or fork, mixing well until mixture is moist. Sprinkle over rice mixture.

Bake 20 minutes. Serve with ice cream, if desired.

popcorn granola
makes 8 servings

  1 cup quick oats
  6 cups air-popped popcorn
  1 cup golden raisins
  ½ cup chopped mixed dried fruit
  ¼ cup sunflower kernels
  2 tablespoons butter
  2 tablespoons packed light brown sugar
  1 tablespoon honey
  ¼ teaspoon ground cinnamon
  ¼ teaspoon ground nutmeg

1. Preheat oven to 350°F. Spread oats on ungreased baking sheet; bake 10 to 15 minutes or until lightly toasted, stirring occasionally.

2. Combine oats, popcorn, raisins, dried fruit and sunflower kernels in large bowl.

3. Heat butter, brown sugar, honey, cinnamon and nutmeg in small saucepan over medium heat until butter is melted. Drizzle over popcorn mixture; toss to coat.

tip: It's simple to make air-popped popcorn without a popper. For 6 cups of popped corn, you'll need about ¾ cup kernels. Place them in a brown paper bag, making sure the bottom of the bag is opened up, and fold the top over three times to keep the bag closed. Microwave the popcorn on HIGH about 4 minutes or until the popping slows to several seconds between pops.

rustic plum tart

makes 8 servings

¼ cup (½ stick) plus 1 tablespoon butter, divided

3 cups plum wedges (about 6 medium, see Tip)

¼ cup granulated sugar

½ cup all-purpose flour

½ cup old-fashioned or quick oats

¼ cup packed brown sugar

½ teaspoon ground cinnamon

¼ teaspoon salt

1 egg

1 teaspoon water

1 refrigerated pie crust (half of 15-ounce package)

1 tablespoon chopped crystallized ginger

1. Preheat oven to 425°F. Line baking sheet with parchment paper.

2. Melt 1 tablespoon butter in large skillet over high heat. Add plums; cook and stir 3 minutes or until plums are softened. Stir in granulated sugar; cook 1 minute or until juices are thickened. Remove from heat; set aside.

3. Combine flour, oats, brown sugar, cinnamon and salt in medium bowl. Cut in remaining ¼ cup butter with pastry blender or two knives until mixture resembles coarse crumbs.

4. Beat egg and water in small bowl. Unroll pie crust on prepared baking sheet. Brush crust lightly with egg mixture. Sprinkle with ¼ cup oat mixture, leaving 2-inch border around edge of crust. Spoon plums over oat mixture, leaving juices in skillet. Sprinkle with ginger. Fold crust edge up around plums, overlapping as necessary. Sprinkle with remaining oat mixture. Brush edge of crust with egg mixture.

5. Bake 25 minutes or until golden brown. Cool slightly before serving.

tip: For this recipe, use dark reddish-purple plums and cut the fruit into 8 wedges.

double cherry crumbles
makes 8 servings

½ (16-ounce) package refrigerated oatmeal raisin cookie dough*
½ cup old-fashioned oats
¾ teaspoon ground cinnamon
½ teaspoon ground ginger
2 tablespoons cold butter, cut into small pieces
1 cup chopped pecans, toasted**
2 cans (21 ounces each) cherry pie filling
1 package (16 ounces) frozen pitted unsweetened dark sweet
    cherries, thawed

*Save remaining ½ package of dough for another use.

**To toast pecans, spread in single layer on baking sheet. Bake in preheated 350°F oven
5 to 7 minutes or until golden brown, stirring frequently.

1. Let dough stand at room temperature 15 minutes. Grease eight
½-cup custard cups or ramekins; place on baking sheet.

2. Preheat oven to 350°F. Beat dough, oats, cinnamon and ginger in
large bowl until well blended. Cut in butter with pastry blender or
two knives. Stir in pecans.

3. Combine pie filling and cherries in large bowl. Divide cherry
mixture evenly among prepared cups; sprinkle with pecan mixture.

4. Bake 25 minutes or until golden brown. Serve warm.

fruit crisp
makes 8 servings

filling

- 6 cups thinly sliced peeled apples, peaches or pears (6 to 8 medium)
- ¼ cup water
- ¼ cup firmly packed brown sugar
- 2 tablespoons all-purpose flour
- ½ teaspoon ground cinnamon

topping

- ¾ cup QUAKER® Oats (quick or old fashioned, uncooked)
- 3 tablespoons firmly packed brown sugar
- 2 tablespoons margarine or light butter, melted
- ¼ teaspoon ground cinnamon
  Nonfat frozen yogurt (optional)

1. Heat oven to 350°F. Spray 8-inch square glass baking dish with nonstick cooking spray.

2. For filling, combine fruit and water in large bowl. Add brown sugar, flour and cinnamon; stir until fruit is evenly coated. Spoon into baking dish.

3. For topping, combine oats, brown sugar, margarine and cinnamon in medium bowl; mix well. Sprinkle evenly over fruit.

4. Bake 30 to 35 minutes or until fruit is tender. Serve warm with nonfat frozen yogurt, if desired.

tip: If using apples, Jonathan, McIntosh, Winesap, Granny Smith, Northern Spy, Greening and Rome Beauty are recommended. One medium apple yields about 1 cup sliced or chopped. If using pears, Bartlett, Anjou and Bosc are recommended.

oat-apricot snack cake
makes 32 servings

1 container (6 ounces) plain yogurt (not fat free)
¾ cup packed brown sugar
½ cup granulated sugar
⅓ cup vegetable oil
1 egg
2 tablespoons milk
2 teaspoons vanilla
1 cup all-purpose flour
½ cup whole wheat flour
1 teaspoon baking soda
1 teaspoon cinnamon
½ teaspoon salt
2 cups old-fashioned oats
1 cup chopped dried apricots
1 cup powdered sugar
2 tablespoons milk

1. Preheat oven to 350°F. Spray 13×9-inch baking pan with nonstick cooking spray. Stir yogurt, brown sugar, granulated sugar, oil, egg, milk and vanilla in large bowl until well blended.

2. Sift all-purpose flour, whole wheat flour, baking soda, cinnamon and salt into medium bowl. Add flour mixture to yogurt mixture; mix well. Stir in oats and apricots until blended. Spread batter in prepared pan.

3. Bake 25 to 30 minutes or until toothpick inserted into center comes out clean. Cool completely in pan on wire rack.

4. Stir powdered sugar and milk in small bowl until smooth. Spoon glaze into small resealable food storage bag. Seal bag and cut ¼ inch from one corner; drizzle glaze over cake.

oats 'n' apple tart

makes 8 servings

1½ **cups quick oats**
½ **cup packed brown sugar, divided**
1 **tablespoon plus ¼ teaspoon ground cinnamon, divided**
5 **tablespoons butter, melted**
2 **medium sweet apples, such as Golden Delicious, unpeeled, cored and thinly sliced**
1 **teaspoon lemon juice**
¼ **cup water**
1 **envelope (¼ ounce) unflavored gelatin**
½ **cup apple juice concentrate**
1 **package (8 ounces) cream cheese, softened**
⅛ **teaspoon ground nutmeg**

1. Preheat oven to 350°F. Combine oats, ¼ cup brown sugar and 1 tablespoon cinnamon in medium bowl. Stir in butter until blended. Press mixture onto bottom and up side of 9-inch pie plate. Bake 7 minutes or until set. Cool on wire rack.

2. Toss apple slices with lemon juice in small bowl; set aside. Place water in small saucepan. Sprinkle gelatin over water; let stand 3 to 5 minutes. Stir in apple juice concentrate. Cook and stir over medium heat until gelatin is dissolved. *Do not boil.* Remove from heat.

3. Beat cream cheese in medium bowl with electric mixer at medium speed until fluffy and smooth. Add remaining ¼ cup brown sugar, ¼ teaspoon cinnamon and nutmeg; beat until blended. Slowly beat in gelatin mixture at low speed about 1 minute or until creamy. *Do not overbeat.*

4. Arrange apple slices in crust. Pour cream cheese mixture evenly over top. Refrigerate 2 hours or until set.

mixed berry crisp
makes 2 servings

1 tablespoon plus 2 teaspoons granulated sugar, divided
1 tablespoon cornstarch*
2 cups mixed berries (thawed if frozen)
½ cup old-fashioned oats
¼ cup packed brown sugar
2 tablespoons all-purpose flour
½ teaspoon ground cinnamon
⅛ teaspoon ground ginger
⅛ teaspoon salt
3 tablespoons cold butter

Increase to 2 tablespoons if using frozen berries.

1. Preheat oven to 375°F.

2. Combine 2 teaspoons granulated sugar and cornstarch in medium bowl. Add berries; toss to coat evenly. Divide berry mixture between two 5-inch heart-shaped pie plates or 5-inch baking dishes.

3. For topping, combine oats, brown sugar, flour, remaining 1 tablespoon granulated sugar, cinnamon, ginger and salt in small bowl. Cut in butter with pastry blender or two knives until mixture resembles coarse crumbs. Sprinkle topping evenly over berries.

4. Bake 20 to 25 minutes or until topping is golden brown and berries are bubbling around edges. Serve warm.

pumpkin silk pie

makes 10 servings

crust

1 cup QUAKER® Oats (quick or old fashioned, uncooked)
¾ cup all-purpose flour
½ cup (1 stick) margarine or butter, melted
¼ cup firmly packed brown sugar

filling

2 packages (8 ounces each) cream cheese, softened*
1 can (16 ounces) pumpkin
1½ cups powdered sugar
2 teaspoons vanilla
2 teaspoons ground cinnamon
½ teaspoon ground nutmeg
½ teaspoon ground ginger
2 cups thawed nondairy whipped topping
¼ cup coarsely chopped pecans (optional)

*To soften cream cheese, place in large microwavable bowl. Microwave on HIGH 30 seconds or until softened.

1. Heat oven to 375°F. Lightly grease 9-inch pie plate. For crust, combine all ingredients; mix well. Press mixture evenly onto bottom and side of prepared pie plate. Bake 12 to 15 minutes or until golden brown. Cool completely.

2. For filling, in large mixing bowl, combine all ingredients except whipped topping and pecans. Beat on medium speed of electric mixer until smooth, about 1 to 2 minutes. By hand, gently fold in whipped topping. Spread filling into prepared crust. Chill at least 3 hours or overnight. Top with pecans, if desired.

tip: Light cream cheese may be substituted for regular, and fat-free whipped topping may be substituted for regular.

apple crumble pot
makes 6 to 8 servings

    1 cup plus 2 tablespoons biscuit baking mix, divided
    1 cup packed dark brown sugar, divided
 1½ teaspoons ground cinnamon, plus additional for garnish
  ¼ teaspoon ground allspice
    4 Granny Smith apples (about 2 pounds), cored and cut
       into 8 wedges each
  ½ cup dried cranberries
    5 tablespoons butter, cubed, divided
    1 teaspoon vanilla
  ½ cup old-fashioned oats
  ½ cup chopped pecans
       Whipped cream (optional)

slow cooker directions

1. Spray slow cooker with nonstick cooking spray. Combine
2 tablespoons baking mix, ⅔ cup brown sugar, cinnamon and
allspice in large bowl. Add apples, cranberries, 2 tablespoons
butter and vanilla; toss gently to coat. Transfer to slow cooker.

2. Combine remaining 1 cup baking mix, oats and remaining ⅓ cup
brown sugar in large bowl. Cut in remaining 3 tablespoons butter
with pastry blender or two knives until mixture resembles coarse
crumbs. Sprinkle evenly over fruit mixture in slow cooker. Top with
pecans.

3. Cover; cook on HIGH 2 hours or until apples are tender. Turn off
slow cooker. Let stand, uncovered, 15 to 30 minutes before serving.
Top with whipped cream and additional cinnamon, if desired.

greek-style meatballs and spinach
makes 4 servings

- ½ cup old-fashioned oats
- ¼ cup minced onion
- 1 clove garlic, minced
- ¼ teaspoon dried oregano
- ⅛ teaspoon black pepper
- 1 egg
- 8 ounces ground lamb
- 1 cup reduced-sodium beef broth
- ¼ teaspoon salt
- ½ cup plain yogurt
- 1 teaspoon all-purpose flour
- 4 cups fresh baby spinach, coarsely chopped
- 2 cups cooked egg noodles

slow cooker directions

1. Combine oats, onion, garlic, oregano and pepper in medium bowl. Stir in egg. Add ground lamb; mix gently. Shape lamb mixture into 16 balls. Place in slow cooker.

2. Add broth and salt. Cover; cook on LOW 6 hours.

3. Blend yogurt and flour in small bowl. Spoon about ¼ cup hot liquid from slow cooker into yogurt; stir until smooth. Stir yogurt mixture back into liquid in slow cooker.

4. Stir in spinach. Cover; cook on LOW 10 minutes to heat through. Serve over noodles.

asian stuffed mushrooms
makes 24 appetizers

24 large mushrooms (about 2 pounds)
½ cup reduced-sodium soy sauce
¼ cup dry sherry
½ pound ground turkey
¾ cup QUAKER® Oats (quick or old fashioned, uncooked)
½ cup sliced green onions
¼ cup finely chopped red or green bell pepper
1 egg white, lightly beaten
1 tablespoon Dijon-style mustard
2 cloves garlic, minced

1. Remove stems from mushrooms; reserve stems. Place mushroom caps in large bowl. Combine soy sauce and sherry in small bowl; pour over mushrooms. Cover and marinate at least 1 hour, stirring once after 30 minutes.

2. Finely chop reserved mushroom stems. Place in large bowl with turkey, oats, green onions, bell pepper, egg white, mustard and garlic; mix well. Drain mushroom caps, reserving marinade. Fill caps with turkey mixture, packing well and mounding slightly. Place on broiler pan. Brush tops with reserved marinade.

3. Broil 7 to 8 inches from heat 15 to 18 minutes or until turkey is cooked through. Serve immediately.

oat-topped sweet potato crisp
makes 8 servings

- 1 package (8 ounces) PHILADELPHIA® Cream Cheese, softened
- 1 can (40 ounces) cut sweet potatoes, drained
- ¾ cup firmly packed brown sugar, divided
- ¼ teaspoon ground cinnamon
- 1 cup chopped apples
- ⅔ cup chopped cranberries
- ½ cup flour
- ½ cup old-fashioned or quick-cooking oats, uncooked
- ⅓ cup cold butter or margarine
- ¼ cup chopped PLANTERS® Pecans

HEAT oven to 350°F. Beat cream cheese, sweet potatoes, ¼ cup of the sugar and cinnamon with electric mixer on medium speed until well blended. Spoon into 1½-quart casserole dish; top with apples and cranberries.

MIX flour, oats and remaining ½ cup sugar in medium bowl; cut in butter until mixture resembles coarse crumbs. Stir in pecans. Sprinkle over fruit mixture.

BAKE 35 to 40 minutes or until heated through.

substitute: Prepare as directed, using PHILADELPHIA® ⅓ Less Fat Cream Cheese.

variation: Prepare as directed, substituting a 10×6-inch baking dish for the 1½-quart casserole dish.

prep time: 20 minutes • **bake time:** 40 minutes

nut roast
makes 6 to 8 servings

  1½ cups unsalted walnuts, pecans, almonds or cashews
    2 tablespoons olive oil
    1 onion, finely chopped
    4 ounces cremini mushrooms (about 6 large), sliced
    2 cloves garlic, minced
    1 can (about 14 ounces) diced tomatoes
    1 cup old-fashioned oats
    2 eggs, lightly beaten
    2 tablespoons all-purpose flour
    1 tablespoon chopped fresh sage
    1 tablespoon chopped fresh parsley
    1 teaspoon chopped fresh thyme
      Salt and black pepper

1. Preheat oven to 350°F. Spray 8×4-inch loaf pan with nonstick cooking spray.

2. Place nuts in food processor. Pulse until finely chopped, allowing some larger pieces to remain. Transfer to large bowl.

3. Heat oil in medium skillet over medium heat. Add onion, mushrooms and garlic; cook and stir 3 minutes or until softened. Transfer mixture to bowl with nuts.

4. Stir in tomatoes, oats, eggs, flour, sage, parsley, thyme, salt and pepper until combined. Spoon mixture into prepared pan.

5. Bake 45 to 50 minutes or until firm and browned. Cool slightly before slicing.

nancy's grilled turkey meatballs

makes 6 servings

- **1 pound lean ground turkey breast**
- **½ cup oatmeal**
- **¼ cup fresh whole wheat bread crumbs**
- **3 tablespoons fat-free or reduced-fat Parmesan cheese**
- **1 egg white**
- **2 tablespoons FRENCH'S® Honey Dijon Mustard**
- **¼ teaspoon crushed garlic**
- **¼ teaspoon ground black pepper**
- **1 cup pineapple chunks or wedges**
- **1 small red bell pepper, cut into squares**

1. Combine turkey, oatmeal, bread crumbs, cheese, egg white, mustard, garlic and black pepper in large bowl. Mix well and form into 24 meatballs.

2. Place 4 meatballs on each skewer, alternating with pineapple and bell pepper.

3. Cook meatballs 10 minutes on well-greased grill over medium heat until no longer pink inside, turning often. Serve with additional French's® Honey Dijon Mustard on the side for dipping.

tip: Combine ⅓ cup *each* French's® Honey Dijon Mustard, honey and Frank's® RedHot® Cayenne Pepper Sauce. Use for dipping grilled wings, ribs and chicken.

prep time: 15 minutes • **cook time:** 10 minutes

mexi-meatball kabobs
makes 30 servings (2 skewers each)

  Nonstick cooking spray
3 pounds lean ground beef
2 cups quick oats
1 can (12 fluid ounces) NESTLÉ® CARNATION® Evaporated Milk
2 large eggs
½ cup ketchup
2 packets (1¼ ounces *each*) taco seasoning mix
1 teaspoon ground black pepper
3 large bell peppers (any color), cut into 60 (1-inch) pieces
60 (4-inch) wooden skewers
  Salsa and sour cream (optional)

PREHEAT oven to 350°F. Foil-line 3 baking sheets and spray with nonstick cooking spray.

COMBINE ground beef, oats, evaporated milk, eggs, ketchup, taco seasoning and black pepper in large bowl until just mixed. Form mixture into 120 (1-inch) meatballs. Place on prepared baking sheets.

BAKE for 15 to 20 minutes or until no longer pink in center. Drain on paper towels, if needed.

THREAD two meatballs and one piece of pepper on *each* skewer. Place on large serving platter. Serve with salsa and sour cream.

tip: Meatballs can be made and baked ahead of time, refrigerated for up to 3 days or frozen up to 3 months and heated prior to serving.

note: Meatballs can also be served individually with toothpicks and dipping bowls of salsas.

prep time: 35 minutes • **cook time:** 15 minutes

broccoli-stuffed tomatoes
makes 4 servings

    4 **large tomatoes (about 1 pound)**
    1 **package (10 ounces) frozen chopped
       broccoli, thawed and well drained**
  2/3 **cup Old Fashioned QUAKER® Oats,
       uncooked**
  1/2 **cup low-fat small-curd cottage cheese**
  1/4 **cup chopped onion**
1 1/2 **teaspoons minced fresh basil or
       1/2 teaspoon dried basil leaves**
    1 **clove garlic, minced**
  1/4 **cup finely shredded Parmesan or Swiss cheese**

1. Heat oven to 350°F. Slice 1/4 inch from stem end of each tomato. Scoop out pulp and seeds; discard or reserve for another use. Arrange tomatoes in shallow 1-quart glass baking dish.

2. Combine broccoli, oats, cottage cheese, onion, basil and garlic in medium bowl; mix well. Fill tomatoes with mixture; sprinkle with cheese.

3. Bake 20 to 25 minutes or until heated through.

> tip: Choose fresh tomatoes by their color and aroma; they should be plump, heavy for their size and firm but not hard. Store tomatoes at room temperature, as refrigerating them will cause their flesh to become mealy and lose flavor.

old-fashioned meat loaf

makes 6 servings

1 teaspoon olive oil
1 cup finely chopped onion
4 cloves garlic, minced
1½ pounds lean ground beef
1 cup chili sauce, divided
¾ cup old-fashioned oats
2 egg whites
½ teaspoon black pepper
¼ teaspoon salt
1 tablespoon Dijon mustard

1. Preheat oven to 375°F. Heat oil in large nonstick skillet over medium heat. Add onion; cook and stir 5 minutes. Add garlic; cook and stir 1 minute. Transfer to large bowl; cool 5 minutes.

2. Add beef, ½ cup chili sauce, oats, egg whites, pepper and salt; mix well. Pat into 9×5-inch loaf pan. Combine remaining ½ cup chili sauce and mustard in small bowl; spoon evenly over top of meat loaf.

3. Bake 45 to 50 minutes or until internal temperature reaches 160°F. Let stand 5 minutes. Pour off any juices from pan. Cut into slices.

hearty meatball stew
makes 6 servings

1 pound ground turkey breast or extra-lean ground beef
¾ cup QUAKER® Oats (quick or old fashioned, uncooked)
1 can (8 ounces) no-salt-added tomato sauce, divided
1½ teaspoons garlic powder
1½ teaspoons dried thyme leaves, divided
2 cans (14½ ounces each) 70% less sodium, fat-free chicken broth
¾ teaspoon salt (optional)
2½ cups any frozen vegetable blend (do not thaw)
⅓ cup ditalini or other small pasta
¼ cup water
2 tablespoons cornstarch

1. Heat broiler. Lightly spray rack of broiler pan with nonstick cooking spray.

2. Combine turkey, oats, ⅓ cup tomato sauce, garlic powder and 1 teaspoon thyme in large bowl; mix lightly but thoroughly. Transfer to sheet of aluminum foil or waxed paper. Pat mixture into 9×6-inch rectangle. Cut into 1½-inch squares; roll each square into a ball. Arrange meatballs on broiler pan.

3. Broil meatballs 6 to 8 inches from heat about 6 minutes or until cooked through, turning once.

4. While meatballs cook, bring broth, remaining tomato sauce, remaining ½ teaspoon thyme and salt, if desired, to a boil in 4-quart saucepan or Dutch oven over medium-high heat. Add vegetables and pasta; return to a boil. Reduce heat, cover and simmer 10 minutes or until vegetables and pasta are tender. Stir together water and cornstarch in small bowl until smooth. Add to saucepan with meatballs. Cook and stir until broth is thickened. Spoon into bowls.

bacon-wrapped pork and apple patties
makes 4 servings

1 pound lean ground pork
¾ cup quick-cooking rolled oats
Salt
½ teaspoon ground sage
¼ teaspoon pepper
¼ teaspoon dried thyme leaves, crushed
⅓ cup applesauce
1 egg, slightly beaten
2 tablespoons chopped green onion
4 slices bacon
1 large tart green apple, cut into thin wedges
½ medium onion, cut into small wedges
1 tablespoon olive oil

In large bowl combine oats, ½ teaspoon salt, sage, pepper and thyme. Stir in applesauce, egg and green onion; mix well. Stir in ground pork until well blended. Form into 4 patties about ¾ to 1 inch thick. Wrap 1 bacon strip around each patty; secure with toothpick. Grill or broil patties 4 to 5 minutes on each side until no longer pink in center.

Meanwhile in small skillet, cook and stir apple and onion in hot oil until tender. Sprinkle lightly with salt. Serve with patties.

*Favorite recipe from **National Pork Board***

mini turkey loaves

makes 4 servings

- **1 pound ground turkey**
- **1 small apple, chopped**
- **½ small onion, chopped**
- **½ cup old-fashioned oats**
- **2 teaspoons Dijon mustard**
- **1 teaspoon dried rosemary**
- **1 teaspoon salt**
- **Dash black pepper**
- **Cranberry sauce**
- **Mashed potatoes (optional)**

1. Preheat oven to 425°F. Spray 12 standard (2½-inch) muffin cups with nonstick cooking spray.

2. Combine turkey, apple, onion, oats, mustard, rosemary, salt and pepper in large bowl; mix just until blended. Press evenly into prepared muffin cups.

3. Bake 20 minutes or until lightly browned and cooked through (165°F). Top with cranberry sauce. Serve with mashed potatoes, if desired.

tip: Ground turkey comes in various percentages of lean. Regular ground turkey (85% lean) is a combination of white and dark meat, which is comparable in fat to some lean cuts of ground beef. Ground turkey breast is lowest in fat (up to 99% lean), but it can dry out very easily. In between these two products, 93% lean ground turkey is available in many supermarkets and is a good compromise that works well in many recipes.

traditional stuffing
makes 9 cups

  2 cups sliced celery
  1 cup chopped onion
1½ tablespoons poultry seasoning
  1 teaspoon sage
  ½ teaspoon salt
  ¼ teaspoon black pepper
  2 tablespoons olive oil
  8 cups fresh bread cubes (white, whole wheat or multi-grain)
  2 cups QUAKER® Oats (quick or old fashioned, uncooked)
  1 cup chopped apple
  1 cup dried cranberries
  ½ cup chopped walnuts
  ¼ cup chopped parsley
  1 can (10¾ ounces) chicken broth

1. Cook celery, onion, poultry seasoning, sage, salt and pepper in oil over medium-low heat 4 to 5 minutes or until tender. Remove from heat.

2. Combine bread cubes, oats, apple, dried cranberries, walnuts and parsley in large bowl; mix well.

3. Add onion mixture and chicken broth. Mix until bread is evenly coated.

4. Stuff into body and neck of turkey. Immediately after stuffing, place turkey in oven and begin roasting.

tip: This is enough stuffing for a 13- to 19-pound turkey. If using a larger turkey, double the recipe and bake any remaining stuffing in a casserole dish for about 1 hour or until warmed through.

turkey and veggie meatballs with fennel
makes 6 servings

1 pound ground turkey
½ cup finely chopped green onions
½ cup finely chopped green bell pepper
⅓ cup old-fashioned oats
¼ cup shredded carrot
¼ cup grated Parmesan cheese
2 egg whites
2 cloves garlic, minced
½ teaspoon Italian seasoning
¼ teaspoon fennel seeds
¼ teaspoon salt
⅛ teaspoon red pepper flakes (optional)
1 tablespoon olive oil

1. Combine all ingredients except oil in large bowl. Shape into 36 (1-inch) balls.

2. Heat oil in large nonstick skillet over medium-high heat. Add meatballs to skillet; cook about 10 minutes or until cooked through (165°F), turning frequently. (Use fork and spoon to turn meatballs easily.) Serve immediately or cool and freeze.

3. To freeze, cool meatballs completely and place in 1-gallon resealable freezer food storage bag. Seal bag; freeze flat for easier storage and faster thawing.

4. To thaw, remove desired amount of meatballs from freezer bag; place on microwavable plate. Microwave on HIGH 20 to 30 seconds or until heated through.

serving suggestion: Top with meatless marinara sauce.

veggie burgers
makes 8 servings

  3 teaspoons vegetable oil, divided
  1 cup sliced mushrooms
  1 cup shredded carrots (about 2)
  ³⁄₄ cup chopped onion (about 1 medium)
  ³⁄₄ cup chopped zucchini (about 1 small)
  2 cups QUAKER® Oats (quick or
     old fashioned, uncooked)
  1 can (15 ounces) kidney beans, rinsed and
     drained
  1 cup cooked white or brown rice
  2 tablespoons soy sauce or ½ teaspoon salt
  1 teaspoon minced garlic
  ⅛ teaspoon black pepper
  ½ cup chopped fresh cilantro or chives (optional)
     Hamburger buns and toppings (optional)

1. Heat 1 teaspoon oil in large nonstick skillet. Add mushrooms, carrots, onion and zucchini; cook over medium-high heat 5 minutes or until vegetables are tender.

2. Transfer vegetables to food processor bowl. Add oats, beans, rice, soy sauce, garlic, pepper and cilantro, if desired. Pulse about 20 seconds or until well blended. Divide into eight ½-cup portions. Shape into patties between sheets of waxed paper. Refrigerate at least 1 hour or until firm.

3. Heat remaining 2 teaspoons oil in same skillet over medium-high heat. Cook patties 3 to 4 minutes on each side or until golden brown. Serve on buns with toppings, if desired.

acknowledgments

The publisher would like to thank the companies and organizations listed below for the use of their recipes and photographs in this publication.

ACH Food Companies, Inc.

Bob Evans®

California Tree Fruit Agreement

Dole Food Company, Inc.

The Hershey Company

Kraft Foods Global, Inc.

National Honey Board

National Pork Board

Nestlé USA

Polaner®, A Division of B&G Foods, Inc.

The Quaker® Oatmeal Kitchens

Reckitt Benckiser Inc.

Riviana Foods Inc.

The Sugar Association, Inc.

Unilever

Wisconsin Milk Marketing Board

index

metric conversion chart

VOLUME MEASUREMENTS (dry)

1/8 teaspoon = 0.5 mL
1/4 teaspoon = 1 mL
1/2 teaspoon = 2 mL
3/4 teaspoon = 4 mL
1 teaspoon = 5 mL
1 tablespoon = 15 mL
2 tablespoons = 30 mL
1/4 cup = 60 mL
1/3 cup = 75 mL
1/2 cup = 125 mL
2/3 cup = 150 mL
3/4 cup = 175 mL
1 cup = 250 mL
2 cups = 1 pint = 500 mL
3 cups = 750 mL
4 cups = 1 quart = 1 L

VOLUME MEASUREMENTS (fluid)

1 fluid ounce (2 tablespoons) = 30 mL
4 fluid ounces (1/2 cup) = 125 mL
8 fluid ounces (1 cup) = 250 mL
12 fluid ounces (1 1/2 cups) = 375 mL
16 fluid ounces (2 cups) = 500 mL

WEIGHTS (mass)

1/2 ounce = 15 g
1 ounce = 30 g
3 ounces = 90 g
4 ounces = 120 g
8 ounces = 225 g
10 ounces = 285 g
12 ounces = 360 g
16 ounces = 1 pound = 450 g

DIMENSIONS

1/16 inch = 2 mm
1/8 inch = 3 mm
1/4 inch = 6 mm
1/2 inch = 1.5 cm
3/4 inch = 2 cm
1 inch = 2.5 cm

OVEN TEMPERATURES

250°F = 120°C
275°F = 140°C
300°F = 150°C
325°F = 160°C
350°F = 180°C
375°F = 190°C
400°F = 200°C
425°F = 220°C
450°F = 230°C

BAKING PAN SIZES

Utensil	Size in Inches/Quarts	Metric Volume	Size in Centimeters
Baking or	8×8×2	2 L	20×20×5
Cake Pan	9×9×2	2.5 L	23×23×5
(square or	12×8×2	3 L	30×20×5
rectangular)	13×9×2	3.5 L	33×23×5
Loaf Pan	8×4×3	1.5 L	20×10×7
	9×5×3	2 L	23×13×7
Round Layer	8×1½	1.2 L	20×4
Cake Pan	9×1½	1.5 L	23×4
Pie Plate	8×1¼	750 mL	20×3
	9×1¼	1 L	23×3
Baking Dish	1 quart	1 L	—
or Casserole	1½ quart	1.5 L	—
	2 quart	2 L	—